GUIDE TO THE QTS NUMERACY SKILLS TEST

PRODUCED BY QTSSKILLSTESTS.COM

written by Tom O'Toole

Second Edition

Written by Tom O'Toole for QTSSKILLSTESTS.COM – www.qtsskillstests.com

Contents

Section 1 – About the QTS Numeracy Skills Test

Section 2 – Mental Arithmetic Topics

Section 3 – Written Arithmetic Topics

Section 4 – Data Handling Topics

Section 5 – Practice Papers

About the Numeracy Skills Test

What Are the Professional Skills Tests?

The Professional Skills Tests are compulsory tests in numeracy and literacy that are required for an individual to gain Qualified Teacher Status (QTS).

At present, candidates are required to pass these tests before starting their ITT training course (e.g. B.Ed or PGCE). Whilst this can add a little bit of pressure up front, it removes the possibility for somebody to complete a 3 year course only to be denied QTS if they are unable to pass the skills tests.

Who Needs to Take The Tests?

Anybody hoping to gain QTS (including in Early Years Education) in England will need to pass the skills tests.

The tests are not required for those training in Scotland, Wales or Northern Ireland.

Why Do I Need to Take The Tests?

The idea of the tests is to assess the numeracy and literacy skills of a prospective teacher in contexts relevant to the profession.

For example, the numeracy test could include questions requiring calculating the cost of school trips, analysis of exam results and scheduling parents evening appointments.

Though some would object that they are not intending to teach Maths or English, the purpose of the tests is not to assess subject knowledge (this will happen elsewhere in the application for Initial Teacher Training), but rather to ensure that all teachers, whatever their specialism, have sufficient understanding of numeracy and literacy to fulfil their professional role in school.

What is the Format of the Numeracy Test?

The numeracy test is taken on a computer at a test centre, and is in many ways similar to a driving theory test. It is made up of two sections: quick mental arithmetic questions that are heard audibly through headphones, and longer questions that are seen visually on a screen.

The mental arithmetic section is the first part of the test. It is made up of a practice question followed by twelve assessed questions; you will hear each question twice. Once you have heard the question, you will be given eighteen seconds to answer it by typing your answer in a box on the screen. You will not be allowed to use a calculator for these questions, but you will have access to a whiteboard to jot down key facts from the questions and to use quick written methods of calculating. The topics you could be asked about are time, money, proportion, fractions, decimals, percentages, measurements, conversions, and combinations of addition, subtraction, multiplication, and division.

The on-screen section of the test is made up of sixteen questions. Seven of these questions will be on interpreting and using written data, and will require you to extract and use information that is given in graphs, charts and tables. The remaining nine questions will be about solving written arithmetic problems by manipulating numbers in a given context. These questions tend to be more involved than the mental arithmetic questions and you will be allowed to use an on-screen calculator as well as your whiteboard for this section. There are a few different formats in which you may be asked to give your answer: you may be asked to type in a single response, choose from multiple possible answers, point and click in a specific place on a chart, or select an answer and drag it to an answer box. Usually there are a few questions in this section that give you a series of statements about the data you are shown and ask you to select which of those statements are true. In this case, you will only get the credit for the question if you tick all the true statements and no false ones.

Overall, you have forty-eight minutes to complete the test (special arrangements can be made in certain circumstances – see below). Each question in the mental arithmetic section is timed, and allowing for the two readings of the question plus eighteen seconds to answer, questions take roughly a minute each. This leaves about thirty-six minutes for the on-screen section of the test. In the on-screen section, there is no time limit per question, so it is at your discretion how much of this time to spend on each. It is possible to skip questions in this section and return to them later if you wish (this is not an option for the mental arithmetic questions).

What is the Pass Mark?

Though the pass mark varies depending on the difficulty of the paper you are given, it is usually around 63%. In real terms, this means you will need to answer 18 out of the 28 questions correctly to pass.

It does not matter how many you answer correctly from each section as long as you have 18 correct answers altogether. You could pass by answering all 12 mental arithmetic questions correctly and only 6 on-screen questions. Alternatively, if you get all 16 on-screen questions right, you will only need 2 correct answers in the mental arithmetic section to pass.

How Do I Book The Test?

All the latest information on how to book can be found on www.qtsskillstests.com

Do I Qualify For Special Arrangements?

If you have had special arrangements in the past for tests or public examinations, you will be able to request them for your Skills Tests.

You may be able to access an alternative version of the test if you have hearing or visual impairments, physical disabilities, dyslexia, or if English is not your first language. This may involve being given extra time, mental arithmetic questions being displayed on screen, or being given paper versions of the tests in large print format.

If you apply for special arrangements, you may be asked to provide proof that you require these arrangements. This could take the form of a report from a medical professional, a SENCO, or an education psychologist, and it will need to accompany your application for the special arrangements.

You can find further information about applying for special arrangements at www.qtsskillstests.com

What If I Fail?

You are allowed to sit the test up to three times; your original attempt plus two re-sits.

If you fail on your first attempt, don't panic.

Try to identify what types of questions you struggled on and work hard at those areas. Work through the different sections of this book and the practice tests, and look at some of the other resources that we recommend.

Don't rush into your second attempt, but work hard, keep practicing, and when you are confidently scoring in the mid-twenties on practice tests then book in and pass on your second (or even third) attempt.

When a candidate does fail for the third time, they are not allowed to take the tests again for two years. During this time, they will not be able to start their course, but it doesn't mean giving up on your teaching dream.

Such a person could use the time to gain other useful qualifications, boost their classroom experience through teaching assistant work, travel the world, volunteer for a good cause and gain the kind of life experience that will only make them a better teacher when they return two years later to sit the tests again.

Passing the Skills Test

Ten Top Revision Tips

1. Start with a Practice Test

There are three practice tests included in this book, and more are available on www.qtsskillstests.com.

Doing one of these tests is a great start to your preparation as it will give you a feel for the kinds of questions you are likely to be asked and will help you see how close you are to being ready to sit the test.

Don't do too many of the practice papers at this point as it may be helpful to have a few to look at later on in your revision that you have not done before.

2. Evaluate How Ready You Are

When you take the test for real, you will need to score 18 out of 28 to pass, but it is best not to take any chances. Based on your score in the practice test, a good rule of thumb for your readiness is:

- 23-28 – You are ready. You should book yourself in to sit the exam.

- 18-22 – You are not far away. You would have narrowly passed this time, but it may be a good idea to practice a little more, just to be sure. Pick one or two topics that you feel the need to brush up on and use more of the practice tests, until you are regularly scoring 23 or more.

- 0-17 – You are not ready yet. Don't worry though; you are only just starting your revision. Prepare a list of the topics you struggle with and work through the relevant chapters of this guide to help you.

3. Develop an Action Plan

Once you have an idea of how ready you are, determine a plan of action to get you to the point of confidently approaching the test. This may include working through this book, taking a course, hiring a coach and/or using more practice test papers to hone your skills.

4 Identify Target Topics

Whilst there is value in refreshing your knowledge on all topics, it is essential to know which kinds of questions you consistently struggle with and to focus your revision on these areas.

5. Work on One Topic at Once

When you have identified a few topics that you want to focus on, it is helpful to tackle them one at a time. It is better to delve into one area until you are really confident in that subject before moving on to the next than to try to learn a little of everything at the same time, only to confuse yourself.

6. Try Practice Questions

Knowledge in Maths is not primarily gained by reading descriptions of principles and methods. These can be a helpful start, but to truly understand you will need to apply that knowledge to solving specific problems. Each chapter of this guide contains practice questions for you to work through, and there are fully worked solutions for you to check your work.

7. Learn Your Times Tables

In the mental arithmetic section, time is of the essence. A lot of the questions require quick calculations and having instant recall of your times tables (at least up to 12×12, and ideally up to 15×15) makes a big difference.

8. Find Shortcuts

When you are doing the mental arithmetic questions, you won't always have time to use detailed methods. Often there are quick shortcuts that you can use to save time (for example, to divide a number by 5 you can double it and divide the answer by 10). Any tricks that you know to make your calculations quicker may prove invaluable.

9. Become Familiar with the Question Types

It is possible that you will be asked something that you are not expecting, but most of the questions follow familiar patterns. If you have a go at all of the practice tests before you go in, then you will already be familiar with most of the questions you are likely to be asked.

10. Consider Coaching

If you are still struggling with certain areas after working through practice papers and the methods suggested in this guide, then you may want to consider hiring a coach or tutor who can work with you on a one-to-one basis.

Ten Top Exam Tips

1. Write Down Key Information on the First Read Through

For the mental arithmetic questions, you will need to make the best use of your time. Use the first time the question is being read to jot down the key information and to be clear what you are being asked to do. This means that you can start working out the answer during the second read through and gain an extra few seconds.

2. Don't Worry About Using a Thorough Method

There are no marks in this test for showing your working. Particularly for the mental arithmetic questions, the key is to get to the answer quickly. As long as you are confident that what you are doing will work, there is no need to jot down all the steps you take. On the other hand, if jottings help you get to the answer, by all means use them.

3. Use the On-Screen Calculator

For the second section of the test you will have access to an on-screen calculator. Clicking the buttons with your mouse can be time-consuming, and you can control the calculator with the number pad on your keyboard, as long as you press 'Number Lock'.

4. Do the Questions You Are Confident about First

In the mental arithmetic section you have to answer the questions in the order they are asked, but in the on-screen section you can answer the questions in whatever order you want. Start by answering the questions that you know how to do and leave any that you are not sure about (you can click 'flag' to remind yourself that you have done so). When you get to the end of the questions, you can click 'review' and return to the questions that you left to have a go at them in the time that you have left.

5. Be Clear what the Question Is Asking

Just because a question looks similar to one you have done before doesn't mean that it is asking exactly the same thing. Make sure you read the questions carefully and are sure what they are asking you to do.

6. Write down Useful Facts

For many of the questions, you will be presented with data in the form of a graph or a chart. It can help if you jot down on your whiteboard the key pieces of data from the chart that you will need to answer the question.

7. Work out Anything You Can

Sometimes you are deliberately not given the information you need to solve the problem directly. When this happens, the question is a multi-step problem, and you may need to work out a couple of other pieces of information from what you are given, which will then enable you to answer the question that was asked.

8. Check Your Answers

If you have time left at the end of the test, it is a good idea to use it to check your answers. It is possible that you may spot mistakes, and these extra marks can make all the difference.

9. Keep an Eye on the Clock

In the on-screen section of the test, make sure you are allowing time for all the questions, and a little extra to check your answers at the end. Spending roughly two minutes on each question is a good rule of thumb. You can monitor how much time is left in the test by using the on-screen clock that is available at the bottom right hand corner of the screen.

10. Start in the Right Frame of Mind

As tempting as it can be to pull an all-nighter cramming the night before the test, it is likely to be counter-productive. You will perform at your best when you are fresh and awake. Make sure you go into the test with a good night's sleep, good meals, and well hydrated, and give it your best shot.

Useful Resources

For a up-to-date resources that can help you pass your skills tests, visit www.qtsskillstests.com

General Arithmetic

The numeracy skills test is comprised of a number of different topics, and this book will address each of those topics in turn, providing you with methods, tips, and worked examples as well as practice questions for you to hone your skills.

In addition to these topics, there are general mathematical methods that you would be expected to be able to use, and which could come up in questions on any topic. Additionally, there will be at least one question in the mental arithmetic section of the test that addresses some of these skills directly.

Addition

Most addition mistakes happen when numbers are not lined up correctly in the calculation. This is especially true when working with decimal numbers.

The key is to start by lining up the decimal points (if you have a whole number, the decimal point will be at the very end of that number).

For example, if you needed to calculate 6.7 + 23 + 1.08, you would start by lining up the decimal points and insert a decimal point at the corresponding place in the answer.

$$
\begin{array}{r}
6\ .\ 7 \\
+\ \ 2\ 3\ . \\
+\ \ \ \ 1\ .\ 0\ 8 \\
\hline
. \\
\hline
\end{array}
$$

You will then be able to add the numbers in each column (starting from the right), carrying where appropriate.

```
          6  .  7

  +    2  3  .

  +       1  .  0  8
      _____

      3  0     7  8
      _____
          1
```

This gives the final answer of 30.78. (Note – because the column containing 6, 3 and 1 added up to 10, the '0' was written into the answer and the '1' was carried into the next column.)

Practice Questions on Addition

Question 1

What is six point five add three point seven?

Question 2

What is twenty two plus nine point zero six?

Question 3

What is one point six five plus one point eight?

Question 4

A teacher wishes to make a display out of three items. The first has a width of one point two metres, the second has a width of one point four metres and the third has a width of nought point one five metres. What is the total width of the display?

Question 5

A teacher needs to work out the total number of tickets sold for a school show. The number sold by each student is shown below.

Annie	21
Bella	17
Carlos	19
Demi	15
Ed	23
Frankie	8
Georgina	23
Harriet	14

How many tickets were sold altogether?

Subtraction

Subtraction also relies on correctly lining up your numbers, using the decimal point as a guide. When you line up the numbers, you may find that there are blank spaces in some of your columns. If this happens, you will need to fill in the blanks with zeroes.

For example, if you need to work out 1.1 – 0.46, then line up the numbers in a similar way to how you would for an addition question.

$$
\begin{array}{r}
1 \,.\, 1 \\
-\quad 0 \,.\, 4 \ 6 \\
\hline
. \\
\hline
\end{array}
$$

There is a blank at the top of the last column, so this will need to be filled with a zero and then you will be able to do the subtraction.

$$0\cancel{1} \; . \; 1 \, 0\cancel{1} \; 10$$
$$- \quad 0 \; . \; 4 \quad 6$$
$$\overline{0 \; . \; 6 \quad 4}$$

This gives an answer of 0.64. (Notice how we 'borrowed' when we had to do a calculation that would give a negative answer, such as 0 – 6)

Practice Questions on Subtraction

Question 1

What is ten point two minus five point eight?

Question 2

What is the difference between seven and zero point seven?

Question 3

What is three point six minus one point seven five?

Question 4

Rick works out twelve point three minus four point two. He then subtracts two point five from this answer. What number does he end up with?

Question 5

A school production brings in ninety pounds and seventy-three pence. Production costs are twenty-four pounds and eighty five pence and the rest is given to charity. How much is given to charity?

Multiplication

You are likely to be asked to multiply numbers in several of the questions on the test. Depending on what type of numbers are involved, there are different methods that you could use.

For all of these methods, it is important to know your times tables inside out. Particularly with the time pressure of the exams, if you are able to recall instantly the basic multiplication answers you will be well on track to answering the questions (if you are able to learn your times tables up to your 15s, this will help as multiplications by 13, 14 and 15 do come up fairly often).

Below is a times table grid to learn the times tables up to 15.

×	1	2	3	4	5	6	7	8	9	10	11	12	13	14	15
1	1	2	3	4	5	6	7	8	9	10	11	12	13	14	15
2	2	4	6	8	10	12	14	16	18	20	22	24	26	28	30
3	3	6	9	12	15	18	21	24	27	30	33	36	39	42	45
4	4	8	12	16	20	24	28	32	36	40	44	48	52	56	60
5	5	10	15	20	25	30	35	40	45	50	55	60	65	70	75
6	6	12	18	24	30	36	42	48	54	60	66	72	78	84	90
7	7	14	21	28	35	42	49	56	63	70	77	84	91	98	105
8	8	16	24	32	40	48	56	64	72	80	88	96	104	112	120
9	9	18	27	36	45	54	63	72	81	90	99	108	117	126	135
10	10	20	30	40	50	60	70	80	90	100	110	120	130	140	150
11	11	22	33	44	55	66	77	88	99	110	121	132	143	154	165
12	12	24	36	48	60	72	84	96	108	120	132	144	156	168	180
13	13	26	39	52	65	78	91	104	117	130	143	156	169	182	195
14	14	28	42	56	70	84	98	112	126	140	154	168	182	196	210
15	15	30	45	60	75	90	105	120	135	150	165	180	195	210	225

In some questions you will be required to multiply two larger numbers. In this case, begin by multiplying the 'units' digit of the second number by each of the digits in the first number. Once you have done this, you can do the same for the 'tens' of the second number (and then, if necessary, the 'hundreds'). When you record the answer for the 'tens', remember to first block off the 'units' column with a place-keeping zero (and when recording the 'hundreds', you will need to block off both the 'units' and the 'tens').

This is best demonstrated with an example. Consider 124 × 23.

The first step is to multiply the 3 by 124.

		1	2	4
×			2	3
		3	7	2
			1	

Next, put a place-keeping zero in the units column and multiply 124 by 2.

	1	2	4
×		2	3
	3	7	2
2	4	8	0

Finally, add these two answers together to get the final answer.

	1	2	4
×		2	3
	3	7	2
2	4	8	0
2	8	5	2
	1		

This gives a final answer of 2852.

Alternative Method

If you prefer, you can break each number up into its hundreds, tens and units and lay them out in a grid. Fill out each cell in the grid by multiplying the relevant two numbers together and then add all of the numbers together.

For the example above, this would work as follows:

×	100	20	4
20	2000	400	80
3	300	60	12

2000 + 300 + 400 + 60 + 80 + 12 = 2852 (the same answer as was obtained using the other method).

If you are asked to multiply decimals together, start by working out the calculation as though they are not decimals and then insert the decimal point. For example, if you needed to calculate 0.45 × 1.7 you could start by working out that 45 × 17 = 765.

To work out where the decimal point goes, count how many digits are after the decimal point in both of the numbers you are multiplying together. 0.45 has two digits after the point and 1.7 has one, giving a total of three digits.

Your answer will need the same number of digits after the point, so in this case, all three digits of 765 will be after a decimal point, giving an answer of 0.765.

Worked Example

What is 1.4 × 2.6?

Firstly, work out the calculation as though the numbers are not decimals.

$$
\begin{array}{ccc}
 & 1 & 4 \\
\times & 2 & 6 \\
\hline
8^{\,2} & & 4 \\
2 & 8 & 0 \\
\hline
3 & 6 & 4 \\
\hline
{}_1 & &
\end{array}
$$

14 × 26 = 364

Each of the numbers had one digit after the decimal point, making a total of two digits after decimal points.

The answer should also have two digits after the decimal point, so it would be 3.64

Answer: 3.64

Practice Questions on Multiplication

Question 1

What is thirteen multiplied by fifteen?

Question 2

What is seventeen multiplied by two-hundred and eight?

Question 3

What is nine multiplied by one point two?

Question 4

What is two point eight multiplied by three point six?

Question 5

A secondary school has fifteen classes of twenty-nine pupils, twelve classes of twenty-eight pupils and one class of twenty-seven pupils. How many pupils does it have altogether?

Division

The best method for division is often known as the 'bus stop' method.

It involves placing the number that you are dividing inside a 'bus stop' with the number that you are dividing by on the outside. Then, starting from the left, divide by each digit in your number, writing the answer on top and carrying the remainder to make the 'tens' that go with the next digit.

Again, an example would help to demonstrate this method.

Consider 684 ÷ 9.

Start by setting this calculation up inside a bus stop.

$$9 \overline{\smash{)}\ 6 \quad 8 \quad 4}$$

Try dividing the 6 by 9.

Because 9 does not go into 6, the answer would be zero and all 6 would carry over to go with the 8, making 68.

$$\mathbf{0}$$
$$9 \overline{\smash{)}\ 6 \quad {}^{6}8 \quad 4}$$

The next step is to divide 68 by 9.

This does not work out exactly, but 9 × 7 is 63, so the answer is seven, and this leaves a remainder of 5 that goes with the 4 to make 54.

$$\mathbf{0} \qquad \mathbf{7}$$
$$9 \overline{\smash{)}\ 6 \quad {}^{6}8 \quad {}^{5}4}$$

Finally, divide 54 by 9. This gives 6, making a final answer of 076, or just 76.

$$\mathbf{0} \qquad \mathbf{7} \qquad \mathbf{6}$$
$$9 \overline{\smash{)}\ 6 \quad {}^{6}8 \quad {}^{5}4}$$

Alternative method

Division and fractions are two ways of saying the same thing. In other words, 684 ÷ 9 means exactly the same as $^{684}/_9$.

You can work out the answer by simplifying the fraction until you have one as the denominator (for more on this, see the chapter on fractions). In this case, we can divide both numbers by 3 and then by 3 again, giving $^{684}/_9 = {^{228}}/_3 = {^{76}}/_1 = 76$.

This alternative method is particularly useful when dividing by decimals. Set up your division as a fraction, and then keep multiplying the top and bottom of the fraction by 10 until the denominator is a whole number. Then you answer the question as above.

Worked Example

What is 36 ÷ 0.4?

Set up the division as a fraction to give $^{36}/_{0.4}$.

Multiply both numbers in the fraction by ten.

This gives $^{360}/_4$.

As the denominator is now a whole number, you will not need to do this again.

Simplify this fraction.

$^{360}/_4 = {^{90}}/_1 = 90$

Answer: 90

Multiplying and Dividing By Decimals

When it comes to multiplying and dividing by decimals, there are a few calculations that are equivalent. Remembering these can save you a lot of time.

- Multiplying by 0.1 is the same as dividing by 10.

- Dividing by 0.1 is the same as multiplying by 10.

- Multiplying by 0.5 is the same as dividing by 2.

- Dividing by 0.5 is the same as multiplying by 2.

- Multiplying by 0.01 is the same as dividing by 100.

- Dividing by 0.01 is the same as multiplying by 100.

Practice Questions on Division

Question 1

What is five hundred and seventy four divided by seven?

Question 2

What is seven hundred and fifty-six divided by twelve?

Question 3

What is five hundred and thirty-one divided by zero point one?

Question 4

A school organises a trip for six hundred and fifty-three children and eighteen staff. Each bus has a maximum capacity of fifty people. How many buses will the school need to hire?

Question 5

What is seven point two divided by zero point zero four?

Rounding

You will often be asked to round your answer to a certain level of accuracy. This may be to the nearest hundred, to the nearest ten, to the nearest whole number or to a given number of decimal places.

If you are asked to round to the nearest ten or the nearest hundred, identify the digit in question and place a partition after that digit.

For example, if you are asked to round 2473 to the nearest hundred, the hundreds digit is '4', so place the partition after this digit.

$$2 \quad 4 \mid 7 \quad 3$$

Look at the digit immediately to the right of the partition.

If the digit is less than five, leave what is to the left of the partition as it is and replace everything to the right of the partition with zeroes.

If the digit is five or more, increase what is to the left of the partition by 1 and replace what is to the right of the partition with zeroes.

In the example above, the digit to the right of the partition is '7', and so because this is greater than five, the number to the left of the partition increases by 1, from 24 to 25 and to the right of the partition 73 becomes 00, giving an answer of 2500.

$$2 \quad 5 \mid 0 \quad 0$$

When you are asked to round a number to the nearest whole number, put the partition where the decimal point is. The process will be the same as above, but instead of putting zeroes to the right of the partition, just delete everything to the right of it.

For example, round 6.25 to the nearest whole number.

$$6 \quad \mid 2 \quad 5$$

The partition would be on the decimal point, so the next digit is a '2'. Because this is less than 5, keep everything to the left of the partition as it is (6 in this case) and get rid of everything to the right of the partition (the 2 and the 5), so the final answer would just be 6.

If you are asked to round to 1 decimal place or 2 decimal places, put the partition that number of places after the decimal point, and then do exactly the same as above.

For example, if you are asked to round 6.25 to 1 decimal place, the partition would be one space after the decimal point (as shown below).

$$6 \;.\; 2 \,\big|\, 5$$

The digit after the partition is a 5, and because 5 rounds up, increase the number to the left of the partition from 6.2 to 6.3. Everything to the right of the partition disappears so the final answer is 6.3.

Practice Questions on Rounding

Question 1

Round seven thousand, one hundred and forty six to the nearest hundred.

Question 2

Round one thousand, eight hundred and ninety-five to the nearest ten.

Question 3

Round eleven point six four to the nearest whole number.

Question 4

Round twenty-four point six eight to the nearest ten.

Question 5

Round seven point three seven to one decimal place.

Solutions

Fully worked solutions to all of these questions can be accessed at www.qtsskillstests.com/arithmetic

Addition

1) 10.2

2) 31.06

3) 3.45

4) 2.75m

5) 140

Subtraction

1) 4.4

2) 6.3

3) 1.85

4) 5.6

5) £65.88

Multiplication

1) 195

2) 3536

3) 10.8

4) 10.08

5) 798

Division

1) 82

2) 63

3) 5310

4) 14

5) 180

Rounding

1) 7100

2) 1900

3) 12

4) 20

5) 7.4

Time

Units of Time

Questions about time come up regularly on the numeracy test. Usually you will be asked to work out how long a sequence of events will take, or to calculate what time an event will start or finish based on knowing how long all of the components are.

These questions can prove tricky because whilst addition and subtraction questions that work in units, tens and hundreds are familiar, time questions don't follow this pattern. When you are dealing with hours and minutes (or minutes and seconds) you need to calculate with blocks of sixty. If you are working in years and months then you will need to use blocks of twelve.

To illustrate the point, think about the difference between the following calculations:

- 130 + 140

- 1 hour 30 minutes + 1 hour 40 minutes.

In the first of these calculations, standard addition methods can be used to give an answer of 270.

The second calculation doesn't work in the same way. It would not be sufficient to give an answer of 2 hours and 70 minutes, because the 70 minutes is more than 1 hour, so the correct answer would in fact be 3 hours and 10 minutes.

Worked Example

A school has three lessons in the morning, each lasting fifty-five minutes, plus a twenty minute break. If the school day starts at eight fifty, what time does the lunch break start?

The first step is to add up the time spent on each part of the morning. The lessons take 3 × 55 = 165 minutes, and when the 20 minute break is added to this, it gives a total of 185 minutes.

Next, convert this answer to hours and minutes. To do this, see how many times 60 goes into 185. Three sixties make 180 with a remainder of five, meaning that the morning session lasts for 3 hours and 5 minutes.

Finally, add this 3 hours and 5 minutes on to the start time of 8:50, so the lunch break must start at 11:55.

Answer: 11:55

Top Tip

As a lot of questions deal with hours and minutes, it will save you time if you learn your 60 times table before you sit the test. The easiest way to do this is to remember your 6 times table and add a zero to the end of each answer.

Alternative Method

Sometimes you might be asked to calculate with times that are just under an exact amount of hours. In these situations, you could round the time to the nearest hour, and then take off the difference at the end.

For example, you may be asked to calculate the total length of a training day that is made up of three sessions, each lasting 1 hour and 55 minutes.

In this question, you could treat each of the sessions as 2 hours and work out $3 \times 2 = 6$ hours. Once you have done this you just need to take off 5 minutes for each session (don't forget to do it for each session – a common error would be to only take off one lot of 5 minutes). This means you need to take away a total of 15 minutes, leaving the overall length of the training day at 5 hours, 45 minutes.

12-Hour & 24-Hour Clocks

You may be asked to give your answer using either the 12-hour clock or the 24-hour clock. It is important that you understand the difference.

In the morning, both clocks show a similar time (though the 12-hour clock would have 'am' written after the time whereas the 24-hour clock would not, and the 24-hour clock would always display the time as four numerical digits). For example, the 12-hour clock would show half past eight in the morning as 8.30am whilst the 24-hour clock would show it as 08:30.

After midday, the 12-hour clock starts counting again (now writing pm after the time), whilst the 24-hour clock keeps going, so quarter past nine in the evening would be 9.15pm on the 12-hour clock and 21:15 on the 24-hour clock. To convert between times in the afternoon, you need to add 12 to the 'hours' value on the 12-hour clock to get the time on the 24-hour clock (and likewise you can subtract 12 from the 'hours' value on the 24-hour clock to get the time on the 12-hour clock for afternoon times).

Unless the question says otherwise, express your answers using the same clock as any times in the question are given in.

Worked Example

Express the time 16:20 using the 12-hour clock.

The time given is after midday which means that it will be a 'pm' time.

To convert an afternoon time, subtract 12 from the 'hours' value on the 24-hour clock.

16 – 12 = 4 so the time using the 12-hour clock is 4:20pm.

Answer: 4:20pm

School Weeks

Sometimes there will be questions about weeks that it would be easy to get caught out by. Remember that in the context of most of the questions on the QTS Skills Test, a week is thought of as a 'school week' of 5 days.

Worked Example

A pupil is set 20 minutes of homework per night. What is the total amount of homework they are set per week?

Remember that pupils will be in school for five days a week rather than seven, so the correct calculation to perform will be 5 × 20 = 100 minutes.

This answer can be converted into hours and minutes. Sixty goes into one hundred once with a remainder of 40, so the total amount of homework given is 1 hour and 40 minutes.

Answer. 1 hour, 40 minutes

Reading Ages

It is possible that you will be asked a question about the reading age of children.

Reading age is measured in years and months and there are a few different ways that this may be expressed. You may be told that a child's reading age is 10 years, 5 months, that it is 10-5, or that it is 10.5.

All of these mean the same thing.

The last one could be particularly confusing as it looks like a decimal and may cause some to interpret it as ten and a half years (i.e. 10 years 6 months). When you are dealing with reading ages, the dot is not a decimal point and the number you are given is simply the amount of years and months.

Worked Example

A pupil who is 8 years and 1 month old has a reading age of 7-8. What is the difference in months between the reading age and the actual age of the pupil?

The reading age of the pupil is seven years and eight months and the actual age is eight years and one month.

The best way to work out the difference between these two ages is by counting up the months to the next whole year.

Because there are twelve months each year, the reading age is four months short of eight years. The actual age is one month above eight years, so this makes the total difference 4 + 1 = 5 months.

Answer: 5 months

Practice Mental Arithmetic Questions on Time

Question 1

A school day is made up of five lessons, each lasting for sixty minutes. If the school decides to change the length of each lesson to fifty minutes, but wants to keep the same total teaching time, how many lessons will there be in the new school day?

Question 2

A teacher wants her class to complete a project that will require two hours of work. Her lessons are fifty-five minutes, with the first ten minutes set aside for a starter and the last ten minutes set aside for a plenary. How many lessons will she need to allow for the project to be completed?

Question 3

A school trip to an aquarium sets off at nine twenty am and needs to be back by two thirty pm. If the journey is fifty minutes each way, how long will the children be able to spend in the aquarium? Give your answer in hours and minutes.

Question 4

A school sports day will last for three hours. If each race requires twelve minutes, what is the maximum number of races that can take place?

Question 5

A school's lunch break starts at twelve thirty and lunch lasts for forty minutes and is followed by two fifty minute lessons, with a fifteen minute break between them. What time will the school day end? Give your answer using the twenty-four hour clock.

Question 6

A student is given thirty-five minutes of homework each school day. In hours and minutes, how much homework is the student given in a week?

Question 7

A school morning is made up of four lessons, each lasting forty minutes, plus a break lasting fifteen minutes. The morning starts at eight fifty am. What time does it finish?

Question 8

A pupil whose actual age is nine years and nine months has a reading age of twelve years and four months. What is the difference in months between the pupil's actual age and their reading age?

Question 9

A lesson begins at ten twenty-five am. The teacher shows a twenty-five minute video followed by a twenty-minute discussion. At what time does the discussion finish?

Question 10

A training day is made up of four lectures each lasting one hour and twenty-five minutes plus a one hour lunch break. What is the total length of the training day?

Practice On-Screen Questions on Time

Question 11

A secondary school day begins at 8:45 and finishes at 15:35. There is a 40 minute lunch break, a 15 minute morning break and a 10 minute afternoon break. The day is made up of 20 minutes of tutor time followed by five lessons. How long will each lesson be?

Question 12

If a school day is made up of three lessons that each last for 1 hour and 45 minutes, what is the total number of teaching hours in a twelve week school term?

Question 13

A music teacher needs to assess each of the students in his class individually. Each student takes 6 minutes to assess, with a 2 minute gap between assessments. Once the teacher has started an assessment he needs to finish it within the same lesson. How many 60 minute lessons will it take him to assess a class of 22 students?

Question 14

This table shows the actual age and reading age of 3 children.

	Actual Age	Reading Age
Ben	7 years, 9 months	8-6
Jess	8 years, 4 months	7-5
Leah	8 years, 1 month	8-9

How many months difference is there between the reading age and the actual age of the child whose reading age most surpasses their actual age?

Question 15

A parents evening is scheduled to start at 16:00 and finish at 19:15. A teacher has 16 parents to see and each appointment lasts 9 minutes. Before each appointment, she spends one minute in preparation for the appointment. The teacher's schedule for the evening is full, with the exception of one break mid-way through the evening. How long is her break?

Question 16

In a language class, a teacher must assess each student in giving a monologue and having a conversation.

Each monologue will take 10 minutes and each conversation will take 15 minutes.

A monologue or conversation cannot be split across two lessons, but the same student can have their monologue in one lesson and their conversation in another.

How many 55 minute lessons will it take the teacher to complete the assessments for all 16 students in her class?

Question 17

A drama company came in to a school to work with 200 pupils. The company worked with pupils in groups with a maximum size of 12.

Each group has one and a quarter hours with the drama company.

What was the total amount of time in hours and minutes that the drama company spent in the school?

Question 18

A reading support specialist works with a group of 6 pupils and he monitors the reading age of those pupils over a six-month period.

Each month he records the reading age minus the actual age for each pupil.

Which pupil had the greatest improvement over the six-month period?

Pupil	Reading age minus actual age (months)					
	Sept	**Oct**	**Nov**	**Dec**	**Jan**	**Feb**
A	4	5	5	6	6	7
B	-1	0	2	3	3	5
C	-3	-4	-3	-1	0	0
D	-5	-5	-5	-4	-4	-3
E	2	4	5	5	6	7
F	11	10	10	11	12	13

Question 19

A reading support specialist works with a group of 6 pupils and he monitors the reading age of those pupils over a six-month period.

Each month he records the reading age minus the actual age for each pupil.

What was the mean improvement in reading age minus actual age per month between December and February for the six students?

Pupil	Reading age minus actual age (months)					
	Sept	**Oct**	**Nov**	**Dec**	**Jan**	**Feb**
A	4	5	5	6	6	7
B	-1	0	2	3	3	5
C	-3	-4	-3	-1	0	0
D	-5	-5	-5	-4	-4	-3
E	2	4	5	5	6	7
F	11	10	10	11	12	13

Question 20

A parents evening was scheduled to start at 4:30pm.

A 20 minute break was scheduled midway through the parents evening.

A teacher had 13 appointment slots, each lasting 10 minutes. Seven of the appointments over-ran, each by two minutes and the parent with the last appointment cancelled.

At what time was the teacher able to leave the parents evening?

Solutions

Fully worked solutions to all of these questions can be accessed at www.qtsskillstests.com/time

Mental Arithmetic Questions

1) 6 lessons

2) 4 lessons

3) 3 hours, 30 minutes

4) 15

5) 15:05

6) 2 hours, 55 minutes

7) 11:45am

8) 31 months

9) 11:10

10) 6 hours, 40 minutes

On-Screen Questions

11) 65 minutes

12) 315 hours

13) 4

14) 9 months

15) 35 minutes

16) 8

17) 21 hours, 15 minutes

18) Student B

19) 1.5

20) 19:04

Money

Total Costs

There are a few different types of money questions that you could be asked on your numeracy test. One of the most common types of question is where you have to work out the total cost of a few things.

In the simplest of these questions, you will be given all of the individual prices and will simply need to add them together. For example, if you want to buy lunch in a school canteen and you choose a sandwich that costs £1.50, some crisps for £0.70, a chocolate bar for £0.60 and a drink for £0.90, then to work out the total cost you would just need to add together these individual costs. £1.50 + £0.70 + £0.60 + £0.90 = £3.70.

It is worth noting that in the example above, all of the prices were given in pounds. It is equally possible that this kind of question could be asked with some of the prices given in pounds and others in pence. For example, in this question you could have been asked to work out £1.50 + 60p + 70p + 90p. If you just added the numbers together you would get the wrong answer (1.5 + 60 + 70 + 90 = 221.5), so you need to start by first converting all of the prices into the same units. You could do this either by converting the 60p, 70p and 90p into pence (you need to divide them by 100 to do this), which would give you the same calculation as above, or you could convert the £1.50 into pence (by multiplying it by 100) to get 150p + 60p + 70p + 90p = 370p. If you choose this second option, you will need to convert 370p back into pounds for your final answer. 370 ÷ 100 = 3.70, so the answer is £3.70, as before.

Other questions may involve more than adding together a list of numbers. For example, you may need to multiply a cost by a number of people (and possibly add on extra costs as well).

Worked Example

A group of 25 pupils go on a school trip to a museum. The cost of entry is £5.50 per pupil, and hiring the coach costs an additional £120. What is the total cost of the trip?

Start by working out the total cost of the tickets. The group will need 25 tickets at a cost of £5.50 each, so you need to work out 25 × £5.50 = £137.50.

Add on to this the cost of hiring the coach. £137.50 + £120 = £257.50

Answer: £257.50

You could also be asked to work out a few different costs and compare which is the best value. This might include adding on additional charges (for example, delivery costs, sales tax or credit card charges) or applying discounts (for example, a percentage reduction or a buy one get one free deal).

Worked Example

A teacher needs to order 30 new textbooks. Supplier A charges £12 per book, plus a tax of 20%. Supplier B charges £20 per book but has a 'Three for the Price of Two' offer on. Which supplier should the teacher use to get the best value for money?

You need to work out the total cost of buying the books from each supplier.

For supplier A, start by working out the cost of each book including tax. 20% of £12 is £2.40 (see the 'Percentages' chapter if you are not sure how to work this out). This means that the cost of each book is £12 + £2.40 = £14.40. The total cost of all 30 books will be £14.40 × 30 = £432.

For supplier B, you need to take the deal into account. For every three of the books you only need to pay for two. Thirty textbooks can be thought of as ten lots of three, so the number of books that you will pay for is 10 × 2 = 20. The total cost of this will be £20 × 20 = £400.

The total cost with supplier B is cheaper than the cost with supplier A.

Answer: Supplier B

Fundraising

Another type of question that is closely linked to the 'total cost' questions is fundraising. You will be given information about a group of pupils who have raised some money and you will need to work out the total amount they have raised altogether.

To start with, you would work out the amount raised by each pupil (this may be the same for all of the students or there may be different students who raised different amounts depending on the question). Once you know this, multiply by the number of students who raised that amount to find the total that those students raised.

The amount of money raised by each student may be a fixed amount or it may depend on how they did in the fundraiser. For example, there may be a sponsored silence where pupils raise 5p for each minute they are quiet. If the students are able to stay silent for one hour, then to work out how much each student raised you would need to multiply 5p × 60 = 300p = £3.

Worked Example

In class 7B there are 13 girls and 15 boys. In a fundraising drive, each of the girls raised 50p and each of the boys raised 40p. What was the total amount of money raised by the class?

Start by working out the total money raised by the girls. To do this, multiply the number of girls by the amount of money raised by each of them. 13 × 50p = 650p = £6.50

Next, do the same for the boys. 15 × 40p = 600p = £6.00

Finally, add together the amounts raised by the girls and by the boys to get the total.

£6.50 + £6.00 = £12.50

Answer: £12.50

Expense Claims

You may need to work out the total expense claims for a journey. Often this will include a 'mileage' claim, where you can claim a certain amount of money for each mile driven. For example, if you were asked to work out an expenses claim for a teacher who travelled 8 miles and was paid 40p per mile, then you will be able to claim 8 × 40p = 320p = £3.20.

One thing to watch out for in questions about mileage expenses is that you will often be told the distance one way but the question will indicate that you are driving there **and** back again, so you will need to work out the mileage claim for the total return journey. To do this you will need to double the amount of miles of the one-way journey.

Worked Example

A teacher is driving to a training event 20 miles away from school and back again. She is entitled to claim 36p per mile. What is the total amount that she can claim for the return journey?

Because she is claiming for the return journey, the total number of miles will be 20 × 2 = 40.

She can claim 36p for each mile, so work out 40 × 36p = £14.40

Answer: £14.40

Income and Expenses

In some questions you may be asked to calculate the total amount of profit (or loss) made on an event. This can be done by finding the difference between the total amount of income from the event (this is the amount of money that is brought in) and the total expenses (this is how much everything costs).

If the income is greater than the expenses, the event will make a profit. If the expenses are greater than the income then the event will make a loss.

Worked Example

A school sells 100 tickets to a show at £1.50 each. They have to spend a total of £40 on costumes, £48 on printing programmes and 25p per guest on refreshments. What was the total amount of profit that the school made on the show?

The income will come from the ticket sales. The total made from selling 100 tickets is 100 × £1.50 = £150.

The expenses will be the total costs of costumes, programmes and refreshments. The refreshments costs 25p each for the 100 guests, so this will come to 100 × 25p = 2500p = £25. Add this to the costs of costumes and programmes. £40 + £48 + £25 = £113.

The profit is the difference between the income and the expenditure. £150 - £113 = £37

Answer: £37

Exchange Rates

Exchange rate questions involve changing money from one currency to another. You will usually be given a conversion factor. This will be something like £1 = €1.60, and it will tell you how much of one currency the other one is worth. In the example given above, each £1 is worth €1.60, so to convert pounds into euros you will need to multiply the number of pounds by 1.60. Similarly, to convert euros back into pounds you will need to divide the number of euros by 1.60

Worked Example

In Belgium, a bureau de change advertises an exchange rate of €1 = £0.60. On a school trip, you want to convert £30 into euros. How many euros would you receive?

The conversion factor is 0.60, and in this question you will need to divide as every 60p is worth €1, so you will need to find out how many lots of 60p make up £30.

Your calculation is £30.00 ÷ £0.60, which will give you an answer of 50.

Answer: €50

Top Tip

By looking at the exchange rate, you can see whether the amount in the new currency should be larger or smaller than the amount in the original currency. If you are unsure whether you should multiply or divide when converting currency, deciding whether you need to make your number larger or smaller will give you a clue what you should do (this is also a quick way to check that your answer is on the right line after you have performed your calculation).

Alternative Method

In a currency conversion question, an alternative method is to divide by the number given for the currency you have, and then multiply by the value for the currency that you want.

For example, if you need to convert £25 into Euros with an exchange rate of £1 = €1.60, start by dividing £25 by the value given for the currency you have (i.e. pounds), so you will do 25 ÷ 1 = 25. Then multiply the answer by the value for the currency you want. This gives you 25 × 1.60 = €40.

Practice Mental Arithmetic Questions on Money

Question 1

A teacher claims expenses for travelling to a training day. The journey is six miles each way and the teacher is entitled to claim forty-five pence per mile. She also claims four pounds and eighty pence for her lunch. How much does she claim in total?

Question 2

Ryan wants to convert fifty pounds into euros at an exchange rate of one pound to one euro fifty-five. How many Euros will Ryan receive?

Question 3

A class of twenty-four children each raise sixty pence per week for charity for two weeks. How much does the class raise in total?

Question 4

Thirty children each raise five pounds to send to an orphanage in Russia. The exchange rate is one pound equals sixty roubles. How many roubles will the orphanage receive?

Question 5

A teacher completes a total round journey of eighteen miles and is paid seven pounds and twenty pence in expenses. How much was she paid per mile?

Question 6

A teacher needs to convert money from pounds to euros for a school trip. She will receive one point six euros for every pound. How many pounds should she convert to end up with two hundred and forty euros?

Question 7

A teacher is entitled to claim forty-two pence per mile for a school trip. The trip is twelve miles each way. How much can the teacher claim for the round trip?

Question 8

What is the total cost of three adult train tickets at two pound sixty-five pence each and four child tickets at one pound fifteen pence each?

Question 9

Twenty-five children are each sponsored five pence per minute to complete a sponsored silence. The children are silent for forty minutes. How much do the children raise altogether?

Question 10

A school production cost a total of one hundred and fifteen pounds for costumes, props and lighting. Eighty parents attended and each paid two pounds fifty for their ticket. How much profit did the school make on the production?

Practice On-Screen Questions on Money

Question 11

On a school trip the exchange rate is £1 = €1.70. A teacher converts £140 into euros, and spends €187. He then converts the rest of his money back into pounds at the same exchange rate. How much money, in pounds, will he get back?

Question 12

The table below shows how much money was raised per student by 6 year 9 classes in a secondary school.

Class	Number of Students	Amount Raised Per Student
9A	28	£1.12
9B	26	£1.37
9C	29	96p
9D	24	£1.09
9E	26	£1.54
9F	30	£1.26

What was the total amount of money raised by year 9?

Question 13

A teacher and a learning mentor were asked to accompany a child to a regional maths challenge. One-way train tickets were £6.40 for an adult and £2.90 for a child. The challenge was 45 miles from the school and, if they went by car, expenses for mileage would be paid at 40p per mile. How much money would the school save on the round trip if they went on the train?

Question 14

In London, the exchange rate between pounds and euros is £1 = €1.59. In Paris, the exchange rate is €1 = £0.64. How many more euros will Jason get if he exchanges £460 for Euros in London than if he exchanges them in Paris?

Question 15

A teacher wanted to buy stickers for her class's exercise books. She was considering 3 different suppliers.

Supplier	Price Per Sheet	Discount	Postage	Credit Card Charge
The Sticker Shop	*12p*	*Every 10th sheet free*	*Free*	*2%*
Stick With Me	*10p*	*None*	*£5*	*1%*
Classroom Supplies	*13p*	*Buy 4, get 1 free*	*£2.45*	*Free*

She wants to buy 500 sheets of stickers and pay with her credit card. She will use whichever company gives the cheapest price. How much will she pay in total?

Question 16

In a fundraising campaign, the average amount of money raised per student is shown on the table below.

Class	Number of Students	Average Amount Raised per Student
Reception	20	96p
Year 1	24	£1.22
Year 2	25	£1.41
Year 3	23	£1.47
Year 4	27	£1.76
Year 5	25	£1.89
Year 6	30	£2.44

$^{1}/_{3}$ of the money raised in the campaign is given to charity.

How much money is given to charity?

Question 17

A classroom resource is advertised at £7.20, after a 20% discount has been applied.

A department has a budget of £100 to spend on the resources.

How many more of the resources can they buy with the discount than without it?

Question 18

A teacher needs to convert £150 into euros for a school trip.

In Dover, the exchange rate is £1 : €1.68

In Calais, the exchange rate is €1 : £0.59

How much better off would the teacher be if he converted his money in Calais?

Give your answer in euros, to the nearest cent.

Question 19

A school orchestra arranged a charity performance and incurred the costs shown in the table below. The orchestra had 300 tickets printed and sold them all at a cost of £4 each. They also sold drinks at a cost of 50p each and 80% of people attending bought one.

How much money was raised for charity?

Item	Cost
Staging	£200
Publicity	£60
Refreshments	£45
Ticket printing	5p per ticket

Question 20

A primary school of 160 children hopes to raise £120 for charity.

Four fifths of the children raised two thirds of the money.

The remaining children are planning to do a sponsored walk.

On average, how much must each child doing the walk raise in order for the school to hit their target?

Solutions

Fully worked solutions to all of these questions can be accessed at www.qtsskillstests.com/money

Mental Arithmetic Questions

1) £10.20

2) €77.50

3) £28.80

4) 9000

5) 40p

6) £150

7) £10.08

8) £12.55

9) £50

10) £85

On-Screen Questions

11) £30

12) £198.82

13) £4.60

14) €12.65

15) £54.45

16) £95.17

17) 2

18) €2.24

19) £1000

20) £1.25

Fractions

How Fractions Work

Fractions, decimals, and percentages are three different ways of expressing the same thing. Each of them can tell you how many parts you have of a whole. This is called proportion. It is important that you know how to work with each in its own right, and that you are able to convert between them.

A fraction is made up of 2 numbers. The top number (known as the numerator) tells you how many parts you have, and the bottom number (the denominator) tells you how many parts there are altogether.

For example, the fraction $^2/_7$ means that out of 7 parts altogether, you have 2. A possible context for such a fraction arising would be if out of a group of 7 students, 2 were eligible for extra support. There are 2 parts out of a total of 7 or $^2/_7$.

Equivalent Fractions

You may sometimes have different fractions that mean the same thing. For example, saying that one student out of every six volunteered to help at an open evening is the same as saying that two students out of every twelve volunteered. The fractions $^1/_6$ and $^2/_{12}$ mean the same thing, so they are called **equivalent fractions**.

Two fractions will be equivalent if you can multiply both the numerator and the denominator of one fraction by the same quantity and end up with the other fraction. In the example above, you can multiply both numbers in the fraction $^1/_6$ by two, and when you do this you will get $^2/_{12}$.

Simplest Form

You will often be asked to give a fraction in its 'simplest form' (also known as 'lowest terms'). This means that you should express the fraction in the way that uses the lowest numbers possible to write it. In the example above, we said that $^1/_6$ and $^2/_{12}$ are two different ways of writing the same fraction. Because 1 and 6 are smaller numbers than 2 and 12, the simplest form of the fraction is $^1/_6$.

To work out a fraction in its lowest terms, you need to see if there is a number that you could divide both the numerator and the denominator by, and still get a whole number as the answer. If there is, divide by that number. This is simplifying the fraction. Then check whether you can simplify your new fraction again. When the fraction cannot be simplified any further, it is in its lowest terms. For example, you may need to write the fraction $^{24}/_{36}$ in its simplest form. You notice that both numbers can be divided by 4, and this would leave you with $^{6}/_{9}$. Now you notice that both of the numbers in your new fraction can be divided by 3, giving an answer of $^{2}/_{3}$. This cannot be simplified any further, so $^{2}/_{3}$ is the fraction in its lowest terms.

Note: it is possible that instead of dividing by 4, you may have chosen a different number to divide 24 and 36 by (2, 3, 4, 6 and 12 all work). As long as you continue simplifying your answer until it can't be simplified any more, your answer will be the same regardless of which of these numbers you initially divided by.

Worked Example

In a school, 45 students choose to take media studies GCSE. The school enter 27 of them for the higher tier. What fraction is this? Give your answer in its lowest terms.

You are considering 27 parts out of a total of 45, so you can make this into the fraction $^{27}/_{45}$.

Next, you need to simplify the fraction. If you divide both numbers by 3, you will get $^{9}/_{15}$. You can divide these answers by 3 again to give you $^{3}/_{5}$.

Because it is not possible to simplify this any further, $^{3}/_{5}$ is the lowest terms, and therefore the final answer.

Answer: $^{3}/_{5}$

Fractions of Amounts

Often you will be given a fraction and asked to work out that proportion of a given quantity. For example, if there are 24 students in a group and $^{3}/_{4}$ of those students are entered for a higher tier paper, you may need to work out how many students this is.

To calculate this, your first step is to divide the total number by the denominator of the fraction (this is splitting the whole up into parts), which in this case would be 24 ÷ 4 = 6. The second step is to multiply your answer to the first step by the numerator of the fraction (choosing how many parts you want). In this example, this will be 6 × 3 = 18.

Worked Example

30 students are invited to a chess club and $^2/_5$ of those students turn up. How many students are present?

Divide the total number of students by the denominator of the fraction.

30 ÷ 5 = 6

Multiply this answer by the numerator of the fraction.

6 × 2 = 12.

Answer: 12

Top Tip

If you are asked to find a fraction of an amount, you will find the calculations much easier if you put the fraction into its simplest form first. For example, if you need to find $^{12}/_{15}$ of a number, instead of dividing the number by 15 and multiplying the answer by 12, you could first simplify the fraction to $^4/_5$ and then you only need to divide by 5 and multiply by 4, which should be much easier and quicker calculations. This can make all the difference on the timed mental arithmetic questions.

Sometimes you will be asked how many people do **NOT** do something. For example, if you know that $^5/_6$ of a class of 24 pupils bring a packed lunch, then you could use this to work out how many do not bring the packed lunch. The first step is to work out how many of the pupils do bring the packed lunch (24 ÷ 6 = 4 × 5 = 20), and then subtract this from the total number of pupils (24 − 20 = 4) to find that 4 pupils do not bring a packed lunch.

Starting Quantities

Sometimes you will need to work backwards. In these situations you are not asked to find a fraction of an amount, but told what the fraction of the amount is and asked to work out what amount you started with. In this case, you need to reverse the process - divide by the numerator and multiply the answer by the denominator.

Worked Example

In a music class, $^2/_3$ of children chose to play guitar. If 18 children were playing guitar, how many were in the class altogether?

Step one is to divide the number you have (18) by the numerator (2) to get 9.

Next, you need to multiply this by the denominator (3) to get an answer of 27 (it is usually apparent from the context of the question whether the number you have been asked to find will be larger or smaller than the number given).

Answer: 27

Fractions of Fractions

You may be asked to work out a fraction of a fraction. For example, you may be told that $^1/_4$ of children in a school are involved in a school play, and $^3/_4$ of those children are in the chorus and then be asked to work out what proportion of children in the school was in the chorus. To do this, you multiply both fractions together, which you can do by multiplying the numerators by each other and multiplying the denominators together to obtain the numerator and denominator of your answer.

Worked Example

In a school, $^1/_4$ of children are involved in a school play, and $^3/_4$ of those children are in the chorus. What proportion of children in the school are in the chorus?

You need to work out $^1/_4 \times ^3/_4$

The numerators of these two fractions are 1 and 3, so the numerator of your answer will be 1 × 3 = 3.

The denominators of these two fractions are 4 and 4, so the denominator of your answer will be 4 × 4 = 16.

Answer: $^3/_{16}$

Practice Mental Arithmetic Questions on Fractions

Question 1

An art teacher invites the twenty-four children in her class to choose whether they will work with paint or clay. Eighteen children choose paint. What fraction works with clay? Give your answer in its lowest terms.

Question 2

One hundred and forty students are on a school trip and three quarters of them are in year ten. How many students from year ten are on the trip?

Question 3

Half of the three hundred children in a school arrive on the school bus. A quarter of the children walk to school and the rest come in the car. How many children come in the car?

Question 4

A school calculates that nine thirtieths of the children in the school have English as an additional language. If there are two hundred children in the school, how many of them have English as an additional language?

Question 5

An English teacher needs to spend one quarter of the lessons in a term teaching a poetry module. He sees his class three times a week, and the term lasts for twelve weeks. How many lessons will the class have on modules other than poetry?

Question 6

In a group of fifty-four A-Level maths students, twelve students are studying further maths. Giving your answer in simplest form, what fraction of students is studying further maths?

Question 7

Two sevenths of the children participating in a sports day won a medal. There were ninety-one children participating. How many children won a medal?

Question 8

To receive grade A on an exam, a student needs to achieve four fifths of the possible marks. Ninety-six marks are needed to get grade A. What is the total number of marks available on the exam?

Question 9

In a French course, half of the marks come from exams and the other half of the marks come from coursework. Three fifths of the marks available from the exams come from a listening test. What fraction of the total marks comes from the listening paper?

Question 10

On a school trip there are fifty-five children and eleven teachers. What fraction of the people on the trip were teachers? Give your answer in its simplest form.

Practice On-Screen Questions on Fractions

Question 11

In a Geography A-Level, $^3/_5$ of the total marks came from the coursework and the rest from exams. In the exams, there were three papers that each had an equal share of the available marks. Part of Paper 2 involved writing an essay that was worth $^2/_3$ of the available marks for that paper. If the essay was worth 16 marks, how many marks were available for the coursework?

Question 12

A head of department asks teachers to provide a sample of books for checking. She wants $^1/_6$ of the books for each year 7 class, $^2/_9$ of the books for each year 8 or 9 class and $^3/_7$ of the books for each year 10 or 11 class.

For each class round your answer up to the nearest whole number of books.

Below is the number of students that a teacher has in each of their classes:

Class	Number of Students
7X	26
8X	29
8Y	23
9X	28
10X	24
11Y	22

What is the total number of books the teacher will need to provide?

Question 13

This table shows the end of KS2 results in English for children at one school.

	Level 2	Level 3	Level 4	Level 5	Level 6
Girls	5	11	16	13	7
Boys	8	17	21		5

The proportion of children who were level 5 was the same for boys and for girls. How many boys were level 5?

Question 14

In a school production, $^3/_7$ of the money raised by selling tickets was used on production costs.

Out of the remaining money, $^4/_9$ was used to subsidise an upcoming school trip and the rest was donated to charity.

£60 was donated to charity.

If tickets were sold for £3 each, how many tickets were sold?

Question 15

There are 40 classes in a school.

$^2/_5$ of the classes have no teaching assistants.

$^1/_8$ of the classes have two teaching assistants.

$^1/_{20}$ of the classes have three teaching assistants.

All the other classes have one teaching assistant.

What fraction of the teaching assistants are working in a class with no other teaching assistants?

Question 16

In a year group of 240 students, there are students studying French, students studying Spanish, students studying both languages, and students studying neither.

Altogether, $^7/_{12}$ of the students are studying French and $^2/_5$ of the students are studying Spanish.

$^1/_3$ of the students are studying neither language.

How many students are studying both languages?

Question 17

A school invites $^1/_4$ of its students onto a skiing trip, and $^3/_5$ of these students attend the trip.

There are 680 students in the school altogether.

The total cost of the trip is a flat fee of £500 plus £90 per person attending.

What is the total cost of the trip?

Question 18

An exam board is trialling six new exam papers.

They want to find the paper that has the pass rate as close to $^3/_5$ as possible.

The number of students in the sample group and the number that passed for each paper is shown on the table below.

Paper	Number of Students in Sample	Number of Students that Passed
Paper U	110	44
Paper V	85	45
Paper W	180	142
Paper X	275	165
Paper Y	165	100
Paper Z	120	80

Which of the papers should the exam board choose?

Question 19

A P.E. department recorded the number of pupils from each year group that attended an optional after-school football practice session.

Year Group	Attendance
Year 7	23
Year 8	17
Year 9	15
Year 10	10
Year 11	7
Total	**72**

Approximately what fraction of the pupils attending the practice was in year 7?

Circle the correct option:

$^1/_6$ $\qquad$ $^1/_4$ $\qquad$ $^1/_3$ $\qquad$ $^3/_8$

Question 20

The pupils in four Science classes all took a test. The fractions of pupils that passed are shown in the table below.

Class	Fraction of Pupils that Passed
Class A	$^{18}/_{30}$
Class B	$^{21}/_{27}$
Class C	$^{20}/_{25}$
Class D	$^{24}/_{32}$

In which class did the greatest proportion of pupils pass?

Solutions

Fully worked solutions to all of these questions can be accessed at www.qtsskillstests.com/fractions

Mental Arithmetic Questions

1) $^1/_4$

2) 105

3) 75

4) 60

5) 27

6) $^2/_9$

7) 26

8) 120

9) $^3/_{10}$

10) $^1/_6$

On-Screen Questions

11) 108

12) 46

13) 17

14) 63

15) $^{17}/_{33}$

16) 76

17) £9680

18) Paper X

19) $^1/_3$

20) Class C

Converting Fractions, Decimals & Percentages

In some questions you will be expected to express proportions in different forms. You need to be confident converting between fractions, decimals and percentages.

When you have a fraction, the bottom number tells you how many the 'whole' is and the top number tells you how many parts you have. With a percentage, you take the whole to be 100 and the percentage you have is the number of parts out of that 100. If you are working with a decimal, you are expressing what part you have out of a whole of '1'.

Starting With a Percentage

When you start with a percentage, you are told how many parts you have out of 100. For example 62% means 62 parts out of every 100.

If you want to convert a percentage to a fraction, you need to put 100 as the denominator and the percentage you have been given as the numerator. In our example, 62% can be written as $^{62}/_{100}$ and can then be simplified to its lowest terms, giving $^{31}/_{50}$.

To convert a percentage to a decimal, you will need to divide it by 100. You do this by moving each digit two places to the right, so 62% will become 0.62.

You will need to take special care with this when you are converting a single digit percentage (such as 8%) to a decimal. Remember you will still move the digit **two** places to the right, giving an answer of 0.08 (rather than 0.8, which would be a common mistake on this kind of question).

Worked Example

Convert 5% to a fraction and to a decimal.

5% means 5 parts out of every 100, so you could write this as the fraction $^{5}/_{100}$. This can then be simplified by dividing both numbers by 5 to get a final answer of $^{1}/_{20}$.

To convert 5% to a decimal, divide 5 by 100, which would mean moving each digit two places to the right and give an answer of 0.05.

Answer: $^1/_{20}$ and 0.05

Starting With a Decimal

If you are given a decimal, you are expressing how many parts you have out of each whole '1'. To change this to a percentage you will need to find parts per hundred, so multiply your decimal by 100. This is the opposite of dividing by 100, so you will need to move your digits two places to the left. For example, 0.55 will be 55%.

Again, be careful if you have a single digit decimal – you still need to move that digit two places. For example 0.7 would be 70% (not 7%). For a three-digit decimal, when you move the digits two places you will still end up with numbers after the decimal point in your percentage, and this is okay. For example, 0.175 would work out to be 17.5%.

To convert the decimal to a fraction, you will first need to decide your denominator. Count how many digits are after the decimal point. If there is one digit, use 10 as the denominator. If there are two digits, use 100 and if there are 3 digits use 1000. For each extra digit, you will need to add an extra zero to your denominator. Use the digits after the decimal point as your numerator. If, for example, your decimal is 0.55, you have two digits after the decimal point so the denominator is 100 and the numerator will be 55. This gives you $^{55}/_{100}$, which can be simplified to $^{11}/_{20}$.

Worked Example

Convert 0.4 to a percentage and to a fraction.

To convert 0.4 to a percentage, multiply it by 100, which would mean moving each digit two places to the left and give an answer of 40%.

Because there is only one digit after the decimal point, when you convert 0.4 to a fraction you would use 10 as the denominator, with 4 as the numerator. This would give the fraction $^4/_{10}$. This can then be simplified by dividing both numbers by 2 to get a final answer of $^2/_5$.

Answer: 40% and $^2/_5$

Starting With a Fraction

When you start with a fraction, you can convert it to a percentage by finding an equivalent fraction that has 100 as the denominator. To do this, you need to multiply both numbers in the fraction by the same thing, and end up with something out of 100. The numerator of your new fraction will be your percentage.

For example, if you need to convert $^{13}/_{25}$ into a percentage, you can multiply both numbers by 4 (you do this because multiplying 25 by 4 will give you a denominator of 100).

$^{13}/_{25} \times {}^4/_4 = {}^{52}/_{100}$, so it is 52%.

If you want to convert the fraction to a decimal, first find an equivalent fraction with a denominator of 10, 100 or 1000. If your denominator is 10, use the numerator in the first place after your decimal point. If the denominator is 100, place the numerator so that it ends in the second place after your decimal point. If the denominator is 1000, place the numerator so that it ends in the third place after your decimal point.

For example, if you need to convert $^3/_5$ to a decimal, you can find an equivalent fraction with 10 on the bottom if you multiply both numbers by 2. This gives $^6/_{10}$. As the denominator is 10, you put the 6 in the place immediately after the decimal point, giving 0.6.

Worked Example

Express $^7/_{20}$ as a decimal and as a percentage.

For the decimal, find an equivalent fraction with 10, 100 or 1000 as the denominator. To do this, multiply both numbers by 5, which will give $^{35}/_{100}$.

Because the denominator is 100, the numerator must finish in the second place after the decimal point, which gives 0.35

The percentage also uses an equivalent fraction with 100 as the denominator, which has already been calculated to be $^{35}/_{100}$, so the percentage can be found by reading off the numerator from the fraction, which is 35%.

Answer: 0.35 and 35%

Fractions That Don't Easily Convert

Sometimes you may need to convert a fraction to a percentage where the denominator will not go into 100. For example, you may have to turn $^{72}/_{80}$ into a percentage.

If you get a question like this, you should start by putting the fraction in its lowest terms and then seeing if you can now turn the denominator to 100. In this example, both numbers in $^{72}/_{80}$ can be divided by 8, giving $^9/_{10}$, which is the decimal 0.9. To convert to a percentage, multiply both numbers in $^9/_{10}$ by 10 to give $^{90}/_{100}$, which is 90%.

There are questions (particularly in the on-screen section) where this will not help. You will need to change a fraction to a decimal or percentage and even if you simplify the fraction, you will not be able to make the denominator into 10, 100 or 1000. For example you may get asked to express $^2/_7$ as a decimal. To do so, use the on screen calculator to divide the numerator by the denominator. 2 ÷ 7 = 0.29 (rounded to 2 decimal places). To convert this into a percentage, the process is the same but you will then need to multiply the result by 100, giving 29%.

Worked Example

Write $^5/_{13}$ to a decimal and as a percentage.

The first step is to check whether the fraction can be simplified. In this case it cannot, so you will need to divide the numbers to convert it.

To convert $^5/_{13}$ to a decimal, use your calculator to divide 5 by 13.

5 ÷ 13 = 0.38 (to 2 decimal places).

To convert this to a percentage, multiply 0.38 by 100.

0.38 × 100 = 38%

Answer: 0.38 and 38%

Top Tip

Working out conversions can be a time-consuming process. It will help (particularly on the mental arithmetic questions) if you have some of the more common conversions memorised. The table below shows conversions that it would be good to know.

If you are asked for a multiple of one of these fractions, you can use the conversion that you have memorised and multiply it by a scale factor. For example, if you need to work out $^3/_8$ as a percentage, you can take the percentage that you know for $^1/_8$ (12.5%) and multiply this by 3 to get 37.5%.

Fraction	$\frac{1}{100}$	$\frac{1}{20}$	$\frac{1}{10}$	$\frac{1}{8}$	$\frac{1}{5}$	$\frac{1}{4}$	$\frac{1}{3}$	$\frac{2}{5}$	$\frac{1}{2}$	$\frac{3}{5}$	$\frac{2}{3}$	$\frac{3}{4}$	$\frac{4}{5}$
Decimal	0.01	0.05	0.1	0.125	0.2	0.25	0.33...	0.4	0.5	0.6	0.66...	0.75	0.8
Percentage	1%	5%	10%	12.5%	20%	25%	33.3%	40%	50%	60%	66.6%	75%	80%

Practice Mental Arithmetic Questions on Converting Fractions, Decimals & Percentages

Question 1

Write five eighths as a decimal.

Question 2

Out of a class of twenty students, nine sign up for an extra revision class. What percentage is this?

Question 3

The pass rate for a test is sixty per cent. What fraction is this? (In its lowest terms.)

Question 4

One fifth of students on a school trip request a vegetarian packed lunch. What percentage does not ask for the vegetarian packed lunch?

Question 5

The proportion of students that got a GCSE grade C or above is zero point five eight. What is this as a fraction in its lowest terms?

Question 6

What is one eighth as a percentage?

Question 7

A student scored thirty-nine marks out of sixty on a test. What is this score as a decimal?

Question 8

Write ninety-two per cent as a fraction in its simplest terms.

Question 9

One eighth of the pupils in a class are entered for a higher tier exam and the rest are entered for foundation tier. What percentage of pupils is entered for the foundation tier?

Question 10

What is five per cent as a decimal?

Practice On-Screen Questions on Converting Fractions, Decimals & Percentages

Question 11

The proportion of children absent in 7 primary school classes is shown in the table below:

Class	Proportion of Children Absent
Reception	*0.15*
Year 1	*4 out of 29*
Year 2	$\dfrac{2}{25}$
Year 3	*9%*
Year 4	*3 out of 20*
Year 5	*0.07*
Year 6	$\dfrac{3}{30}$

Which two classes have the same proportion of children absent?

Question 12

The numbers of students from each class in year 9 who are participating in a careers visit are shown in the table below.

Class	Total Number of Students	Number of Participating Students
9A	27	10
9B	31	8
9C	28	11
9D	26	12
9E	27	11
9F	28	9
9G	29	8

What percentage of students that are not participating? Give your answer to the nearest whole number.

Question 13

$^3/_8$ of the marks available for a science exam come from coursework. Of these, $^1/_4$ comes from a practical write up. What percentage of the total marks available comes from the practical write up?

Question 14

On a school trip to a museum there are 26 children and 7 adults.

The prices of admission are shown below.

Adults	**£5.40**
Children	**£3.10**

What proportion of the money spent pays for adult tickets?

Give your answer as a decimal, rounded to two decimal places.

Question 15

The proportion of students achieving each grade in a GCSE Physics exam is shown below.

A*	A	B	C	D	E	F	G	U
	$\dfrac{2}{23}$	14%	$\dfrac{5}{19}$	19%	0.12	$\dfrac{1}{14}$	0.03	2%

What percentage of students got a grade A*?

Give your answer to the nearest whole number.

Question 16

To achieve a grade C in a GCSE foundation tier exam, students need to achieve 75% of the total marks available across 2 papers (both papers carry the same number of marks).

A student was confident that they achieved $^3/_5$ of the available marks on paper 1.

What percentage does the student need to score on paper 2 to achieve a grade C?

Question 17

In a school, 22% of students in years 7-9 have a free school lunch and 17% of students in years 10 and 11 have a free school lunch.

There is the same number of students in each school year.

What proportion of students in the school has a free school lunch?

Give your answer as a fraction in simplest form.

Question 18

A teacher compiles a test with a total of 100 marks. He wants to compare performance in this test with a previous test that had 80 marks.

To compare marks out of 100 to marks out of 80, he should multiply by: *(circle the correct answer)*

0.08	*0.8*	*1.25*	*1.8*	*2.5*

Question 19

This table shows the humanities subjects that year 9 students at two schools chose to study.

School	History Only	Geography Only	Both Humanities
Beachside School	38	22	30
Hillside School	17	21	

The proportion of students that studied both humanities was the same at both schools.

How many students studied both subjects at Hillside School?

Question 20

Six primary schools each reported the proportion of students that achieved Level 5 in English at the end of KS2.

The colleges expressed the proportions using fractions, decimals and percentages.

College	Proportion
Woodside School	0.35
Hillside School	36%
Lakeside School	27 out of 60
Beachside School	$^2/_5$
Moorside School	0.4
Riverside School	$^{11}/_{25}$

Which school had the greatest proportion of pupils achieving level 5?

Solutions

Fully worked solutions to all of these questions can be accessed at www.qtsskillstests.com/FDP

Mental Arithmetic Questions

1) 0.625

2) 45%

3) $^3/_5$

4) 80%

5) $^{29}/_{50}$

6) 12.5%

7) 0.65

8) $^{23}/_{25}$

9) 87.5%

10) 0.05

On-Screen Questions

11) Reception & Year 4

12) 65%

13) 9.375%

14) 0.32

15) 8%

16) 90%

17) $^1/_5$

18) 0.8

19) 19

20) Lakeside School

Percentages

Amounts Out of 100

Questions on percentages are very common in the QTS skills test. There are a few skills you need to master to succeed with the percentages questions. The key idea behind each of these skills is that a percentage tells you how many out of every 100 something applies to.

You will probably be asked to find a percentage of an amount. For example, you may be told that there are 800 students in a school and that 40% of those students chose to take part in an optional sponsored read-a-thon to raise money for charity. You would then be asked to work out how many students took part.

40% tells you that 40 students took part out of every 100 in the school, so start by working out how many 100s of students there are. We are told in the question that altogether there are 800 students, so $800 \div 100 = 8$. In each of these hundreds there are 40 participants, so 8×40 will give you the final answer of 320 students.

You may be asked percentage questions like this with harder numbers (especially in the on-screen section where you are able to use a calculator) and the same method will work, even though your answers will sometimes be long decimals.

Worked Example

A local authority works with 1300 primary schools. The authority chooses 15% of the schools to trial a new healthy meals programme. How many schools are included in the trial?

The idea of this question is to work out 15% of 1300.

Because 15% means 15 out of every 100, you need to work out how many lots of 100 there are in 1300.

$1300 \div 100 = 13$.

For each of these 13 hundreds, 15 schools will be chosen, so the total number of schools will be 13 × 15 = 195.

Answer: 195

Building Blocks

Often, especially in the mental arithmetic section, there may not be time to use the method outlined above (particularly when the starting number is not a multiple of 100, as this would leave you needing to multiply decimals – which is hard to do quickly).

There are some percentages that there are easy shortcuts to find. You can use these as 'building blocks' to find other percentages.

- To find 50% you halve the total number (because 50 is half of 100).

- To find 25%, halve the total number and then halve your answer (because 25 is half of 50).

- To find 10%, divide the total number by 10 (because 10 is a tenth of 100).

- To find 30%, work out 10% then multiply by 3. (You can use a similar method to find any multiple of 10%.)

- To find 5%, work out 10% then halve it (because 5 is half of 10).

- To find 1% divide the total number by 100.

Worked Example

There are 80 children in an infant school. 35% of these students go home for lunch. How many children is this?

You can work out 35% by finding building blocks that are easy to work out and add up to 35.

You could do 25% + 10% or you could do 10% + 10% + 10% + 5%.

If you use the first method, find 25% by halving the total number then halving the answer. 80 ÷ 2 = 40 ÷ 2 = 20 children. Then find 10% by dividing the total number by 10.

80 ÷ 10 = 8.

So 25% + 10% would be 20 + 8 = 28 children.

If you use the second method, find 10% by dividing the total number by ten.

80 ÷ 10 = 8.

Find 5% by halving this answer.

8 ÷ 2 = 4.

So 10% + 10% + 10 % + 5% = 8 + 8 + 8 + 4 = 28 children.

Answer: 28

Top Tip

Remember that the total percentage will always be 100%, so the percentage that do something and the percentage that do not do it will add up to 100. If you know that 17% of people do something, then you can find the percentage that do not by subtracting this from 100% to get 100% - 17% = 83%.

Starting Amounts

It is possible that you will be asked a question where the percentage of an amount has already been worked out and you need to work out the starting quantity.

For example, if 25% of a class are away on a trip and 6 students are away, you may need to work out the total size of the class. In this case you would reverse the process for how you would find 25%. Usually you would halve and then halve again, but because you are working backwards you would double and then double again. 6 × 2 = 12 × 2 = 24 children in the class. In any question like this, you can work backwards through your calculations to find the original amount.

Worked Example

30% of the children in a class are chosen to receive an award in an assembly. Altogether, 9 children are chosen. How many children are in the class?

30% is the same as three lots of 10%, so one lot of 10% will be 9 ÷ 3 = 3.

If you knew the total size of the class, you would need to divide it by 10 to find 10%.

Because you already know 10%, you need to reverse this process and multiply by 10 to find the full size of the class.

3 × 10 = 30.

Answer: 30

Expressing Percentages

It is possible that you will be asked to work out what a percentage is when you are told how many people do something. In the worked example above, it is possible that the question could have told you that 28 children out of 80 went home for lunch and asked you to calculate what percentage this is.

The method for doing this is to turn the number you have been given into a fraction, which would be $^{28}/_{80}$, and then simplify this fraction to its lowest terms by dividing both numbers by 4 to give $^{7}/_{20}$. You can then turn this into an equivalent fraction with a denominator of 100 by multiplying both numbers by 5 to give $^{35}/_{100}$, or 35%. More detail is given on this method in the previous chapter (converting fractions, decimals and percentages).

Worked Example

In a school there are 45 classes. 27 of those classes are in the upper school. What percentage of classes are in the upper school?

Start by writing the fraction of classes in the upper school. 27 out of 45 can be written as $^{27}/_{45}$.

Next, simplify this fraction by dividing both numbers by 9 to get $^{3}/_{5}$.

Now make this a fraction with 100 as the denominator by multiplying both numbers by 20, which will give $^{60}/_{100}$, which is 60%.

Answer: 60%

Percentage Increase or Decrease

Some questions ask you to increase or decrease a quantity by a specified percentage. In this case, work out the percentage that has been specified and then either add it on to the original amount (if it is a percentage increase question) or take it away from the original amount (if it is a percentage decrease question).

Worked Example

In a school, if 60 students have achieved grade C in GCSE Spanish, but this is estimated to go up by 20% after a re-sit, how many students can the school expect will get their grade C?

You will need to start by working out 20% of 60. 10% would be 60 ÷ 10 = 6, so 20% would be 6 × 2 = 12 students. Because the question is about an increase of 20% you need to add these 12 to the original 60, giving a total of 72 students.

Answer: 72

It is also possible that you will be asked to calculate what percentage something has increased by. For example, if 20 students enrolled for A-Level history in 2013, and 32 students enrolled in 2014, you may be asked what the percentage increase is. You would do this by making a fraction with the difference between the two numbers as the numerator and the original number as the denominator.

In this case the difference between 20 and 32 is 12, and the original number was 20, so our fraction is $^{12}/_{20}$, which can then be converted into a percentage by multiplying both numbers by 5 to give $^{60}/_{100}$ or 60%.

Percentage Points

Sometimes you may encounter questions that refer to 'percentage points'. There is nothing to be concerned about if this happens. If is simply asking you to compare the two percentages directly. So if you need to find how many percentage points is the difference between 60% and 75%, the answer would be 75 – 60 = 15 percentage points. Be careful to take note whether you are asked to find percentage increase or percentage points increase. They are usually different.

Worked Example

Out of a class of 25 students, 12 pass a practice test. The teacher is targeting an increase of 20 percentage points in the number of students passing the final exam compared to the practice test. How many students will need to pass to meet the teacher's target?

Start by working out what percentage of students passed the practice test. The fraction that passed is $^{12}/_{25}$ and this can be converted to a percentage by multiplying both numbers in the fraction by 4 to get $^{48}/_{100}$, which is 48%.

For an increase of 20 percentage points, the percentage passing the final exam will need to be 48% + 20% = 68%.

Work out 68% of 25.

25 ÷ 100 = 0.25 × 68 = 17

Answer: 17

Practice Mental Arithmetic Questions on Percentages

Question 1

In a writing contest, there are prizes for the top fifteen per cent of students. If one hundred and eighty students enter, how many will win a prize?

Question 2

Out of the thirty-six laptops in a computer room, nine have new software. What percentage of computers do not have the new software?

Question 3

A school needs to buy a new projector and is quoted two hundred pounds plus a delivery charge of seventeen point five per cent. How much will the projector cost including the delivery charge?

Question 4

A teaching assistant spends twenty per cent of his contact time supporting one boy. If he works with the boy for four hours per week, what is his total contact time?

Question 5

Forty three per cent of a Maths exam is focussed on algebra and twenty nine per cent is about shape. The rest is about data handling. What percentage of the exam is about data handling?

Question 6

Twenty-five students take an exam and eighty per cent of them pass. How many students do not pass the exam?

Question 7

Fifteen per cent of children in a school are invited to participate in an activities day. There are three hundred and forty children in the school. How many children are invited to participate?

Question 8

In a school, there are one hundred and eighty children. Forty five per cent of children arrive in the car, twenty per cent of children take the bus and the rest walk. How many children walk to school?

Question 9

A student scored sixty-five per cent on a spelling test. If she scored twenty-six marks, what was the total number of marks available for the test?

Question 10

A student scored eighteen marks out of fifty on a test. They were allowed to re-sit the exam and improved their score by ten percentage points. What was their score on the re-sit?

Practice On-Screen Questions on Percentages

Question 11

The following table shows the percentage of students from 6 different schools who achieved 5 or more A*-C grades at GCSE in 2012 and 2013.

	2012	**2013**
School A	40%	46%
School B	62%	70%
School C	57%	55%
School D	58%	59%
School E	60%	49%
School F	71%	73%

Which school had the largest percentage increase in the proportion of students who got 5 or more A*-C grades at GCSE from 2012 to 2013?

Question 12

An exam was out of 70 marks and the scores of 8 students are shown below.

Student A	Student B	Student C	Student D	Student E	Student F	Student G	Student H
48	51	32	64	55	53	62	37

The minimum percentages required for each grade are below.

A*	A	B	C	D	E	F	G
90%	80%	70%	60%	50%	40%	30%	20%

What was the most common grade?

Question 13

In a school there are 920 students. 7.5% of the students are away on work experience.

Of the remaining students 112 are chosen to participate in a media workshop.

What percentage is this of the remaining students? Give your answer to the nearest whole number.

Question 14

This table shows the number of students in 6 schools that passed an exam, and what percentage this was of the number that took the exam.

	School A	School B	School C	School D	School E	School F
Number of Passes	136	231	182	108	207	224
% Passes	17%	21%	14%	9%	23%	16%

Which school had the highest number of students that took the exam?

Question 15

This table shows the number of students in 6 schools that passed an exam, and what percentage this was of the number that took the exam.

	School A	School B	School C	School D	School E	School F
Number of Passes	136	231	182	108	207	224
% Passes	17%	21%	14%	9%	23%	16%

What was the overall percentage of students that passed the exam? Give your answer to the nearest whole number.

Question 16

A primary school gave a group of students tests at the beginning and end of a term. The school set students a target of improving by 10 or more percentage points over the term.

The test at the beginning of the term had a maximum of 20 marks and the test at the end of term had a maximum of 25 marks.

The scores of the students are recorded below.

	Start of Term Score	End of Term Score
Student A	14	19
Student B	10	12
Student C	11	22
Student D	16	13
Student E	12	18
Student F	15	15
Student G	18	24
Student H	8	11
Student I	16	23
Student J	13	18

Which students achieved the target that the school had set?

Question 17

The end of KS3 level achieved in Science by a cohort of students is shown in the table.

Level	3	4	5	6	7	8
Number of Students	11	28	51	62	25	4

What percentage of the students achieved level 6 or above? Give your answer as a percentage to 1 decimal place.

Question 18

A Maths teacher gave a group of students two mental arithmetic tests a few weeks apart and recorded the results in the table below.

	Student's Score (out of 40)	
Student	**Test 1**	**Test 2**
A	25	28
B	22	22
C	19	18
D	26	32
E	22	34
F	17	18
G	21	25
H	19	19
I	15	13
J	17	23

Which student(s) achieved a score in Test 2 that was more than 10 percentage points higher than their score in Test 1?

Question 19

In 2015, out of 96 FE colleges in a Local Education Authority, 30 were rated as outstanding.

By 2017, this figure had increased by 6.25 percentage points.

How many colleges were rated as outstanding in 2017?

Question 20

The table below shows the number of students achieving each grade in A-Level Chemistry at 5 different schools.

Grade	A*	A	B	C	D	E	U
Woodside School	3	8	14	19	15	6	2
Hillside School	4	10	10	24	22	8	3
Beachside School	3	9	13	15	18	10	1
Riverside School	2	11	10	16	24	5	5
Moorside School	6	17	12	17	10	4	0

Across all 3 schools, what percentage of students achieved a grade B or above?

Give your answer as a percentage to one decimal place.

Solutions

Fully worked solutions to all of these questions can be accessed at www.qtsskillstests.com/percentages

Mental Arithmetic Questions

1) 27

2) 75%

3) £235

4) 20 hours

5) 28%

6) 5

7) 51

8) 63

9) 40

10) 23

On-Screen Questions

11) School A

12) Grade B

13) 13%

14) School F

15) 16%

16) Students C, E & I

17) 50.3%

18) Students D, E & J

19) 36

20) 37.1%

Measurements

Types of Measures

Measurements questions will often require you to convert something measured in one kind of unit into a different kind of unit. This could involve converting a distance, a weight or a capacity.

There are two different systems of measurement that you need to be aware of. Most measurements that you encounter will use the metric system, which is designed to make the conversions as easy as possible. However, you may also need to work with a few of the older 'imperial' measures, and you may be asked to convert between metric and imperial measurements.

When you are working with measures of **distance**, the metric measures that you are likely to encounter are kilometres, metres, centimetres and millimetres. The imperial measure of distance that you are most likely to encounter is miles.

When working with **weight**, you are likely to use the metric measures of kilograms and grams.

For **capacity**, you will be working with the metric measures of litres and millilitres. It is also possible that you will encounter the imperial measure of gallons.

Converting Metric Units

Since the 1970s, the UK has used the metric system of measures. This system is designed to make conversions easier because you will be multiplying and dividing by 10, 100 and 1000 (rather than 12, 14 and 16 as in the old system).

In the metric system, there is a base unit for each type of measurement, that is then scaled up or down by attaching a prefix to that unit.

Common base units include 'metre' for length, 'gram' for weight and 'litre' for capacity.

There are prefixes for these base units that can scale them up or down by any power of ten. By combining the prefix with the base unit you can see exactly what to scale the base unit up or down by.

- **KILO** – means that you have 1000 lots of the base unit. For example, a kilometre is a thousand metres and a kilogram is a thousand grams.

- **CENTI** – means that the base unit is split into 100 parts. For example, a hundred centimetres make a metre.

- **MILLI** – means that the base unit is split into 1000 parts. For example, a thousand milligrams make a gram and a thousand millilitres make a litre.

When you are trying to convert between two units that both have different prefixes, you can use these prefixes to work out what to multiply by. For example, to convert from centimetres into millimetres, you can see that 'centi' splits a metre into 100 parts and 'milli' splits a metre into 1000 parts, so you can work out that each centimetre is worth 1000 ÷ 100 = 10 millimetres.

Worked Example

How many grams are there in 2.5 kilograms?

The prefix 'kilo' means that you have a thousand lots of the base unit, so each kilogram is worth 1000 grams.

As you have 2.5kg, this will be worth 2.5 × 1000 = 2500g

Answer: 2500g

There are some common metric conversions that crop up frequently, and it is a good idea to try to memorise these conversions.

- 1 kilometre (km) = 1000 metres (m)

- 1 metre (m) = 100 centimetres (cm) = 1000 millimetres (mm)

- 1 centimetre (cm) = 10 millimetres (mm)

- 1 kilogram (kg) = 1000 grams (g)

- 1 litre (L or l) = 1000 millilitres (mL or ml) = 1000 cubic centimetres (cm^3)

Top Tip

Sometimes you may need to do multiple conversions before you can get your answer. For example, when applying a scale factor to a map you may be converting from centimetres to kilometres. Instead of trying to do this all in one go, it is better to find an intermediate step that would make the calculations easier (in this case you would convert from centimetres into metres, and then from metres into kilometres).

Converting Other Units

When you are converting imperial or other units, the conversion will not usually be a case of scaling up by a power of 10, but there will be some other conversion factor between the two units.

The method for converting measurements is the same as the method for converting currencies that was outlined in the chapter on money. You need to divide the number you are given by the part of the conversion rate that is in the same units, and then multiply the answer by the other number in the conversion rate.

For most conversions of this type you will be given the scale factor, but the one conversion that arises quite often that you should know is converting from miles to kilometres.

- 5 miles = 8 kilometres

Sometimes you may be given a conversion that you have never seen before. If this happens, don't panic. You will be given information in the question about the conversion rate, and the same methods will apply that you have used on other conversions.

Worked Example

Given that 5 miles is equivalent to 8 kilometres, how many kilometres is 35 miles?

You will need to divide the 35 by the part of the conversion rate that is in the same units.

Because 35 is given in miles, this means you will need to divide by 5.

35 ÷ 5 = 7

The next step is to multiply this answer by the part of the conversion rate that is in the units you want.

Because you want your answer to be in kilometres, you must multiply by 8.

This gives an answer of 7 × 8 = 56km.

Answer: 56km

Speed, Distance and Time

Sometimes questions ask about speed. To calculate speed, you need to divide the distance you are travelling by the time the journey will take. If you are given speed, then you can find distance by multiplying speed and time together, and if you want to find the time taken you divide the distance by the speed.

This is summarised below:

- Speed = Distance ÷ Time

- Distance = Speed × Time

- Time = Distance ÷ Speed

Note that sometimes the time that you are working with will not work out to be a whole number of hours. For example, if you travel 90 kilometres in 2 hours 15 minutes and want to work out the speed. In this case, you can't use 2.15 as the time, because hours and minutes don't translate directly to decimals. Instead, you would need to work out the total time in minutes (60 + 60 + 15 = 135) and divide this by 60 to get the time in hours (135 ÷ 60 = 2.25), so to find the speed your calculation would be 90 ÷ 2.25 = 40km/h.

Worked Example

On the way back from a school trip, the coach is due to be back at school at 8:30pm.

If the distance to be travelled is 270 miles and the coach will travel at an average speed of 60 miles per hour, what is the latest time the coach can set off back?

You will need to work out the time the journey will take, so to do this you calculate distance ÷ speed.

The distance is 270 miles and the speed is 60 miles per hour.

270 ÷ 60 = 4.5.

Next, convert 4.5 hours to hours and minutes. Start by multiplying by 60 to find the time in minutes.

4.5 × 60 = 270 minutes.

Now convert this to hours and minutes.

270 minutes = 4 hours, 30 minutes.

The coach will need to set off 4 hours, 30 minutes before 8:30pm, which will be 4pm.

Answer: 4pm

Practice Mental Arithmetic Questions on Measurements

Question 1

A piece of wood that is three metres long is cut into six equal sections. How long (in centimetres) is each section?

Question 2

Using a conversion rate of five miles equals eight kilometres, convert ninety-six kilometres into miles.

Question 3

Using a conversion of one kilogram equals two point two pounds, how many pounds are in 6 kilograms?

Question 4

Two students measure their art projects. The first is one metre, twenty centimetres. The second is seven hundred and fifty millimetres. What is the difference in length between the two projects? Give your answer in centimetres.

Question 5

To find the area of a square, multiply the side length by itself. What is the area of a square with side length thirteen centimetres?

Question 6

For a school trip, a coach travels one hundred and five kilometres at an average speed of forty-five kilometres per hour. In hours and minutes, how long will the journey take?

Question 7

A map is drawn at the scale of one to twenty thousand. What is the distance in kilometres between two buildings that are six centimetres apart on the map?

Question 8

A teacher shares one point four litres of juice between eight children. How many millilitres of juice does each child receive?

Question 9

What is the average speed in kilometres per hour of a coach that drives twenty kilometres in fifteen minutes?

Question 10

How many millimetres are there in a quarter of a metre?

Practice On-Screen Questions on Measurements

Question 11

A teacher is entitled to claim 40p per mile petrol expenses.

Whilst driving in the Netherlands, she drives 120 kilometres.

Given that 5 miles = 8 kilometres, how much will she be able to claim?

Question 12

A school takes a group of students on a trip to London.

The trip is 140 kilometres each way.

On the outbound journey the average speed is 50 miles per hour.

The trip is due to leave at 9am and return at 3pm and the group will need to spend 2 hours in a museum plus 15 minutes for lunch.

Given that 5 miles is 8 kilometres, what is the minimum speed for the return journey that will get the group back on time?

Give your answer in miles per hour.

Question 13

Temperatures can be converted from Celsius to Fahrenheit by multiplying them by 1.8 and adding 32 to the answer.

Convert 7.6 degrees Celsius into Fahrenheit.

Question 14

On a school sports day, an athlete was measured as running 100m in 12 seconds.

Calculate his speed in kilometres per hour.

Question 15

A map has a scale of 1cm : 25 miles.

On the map, the distance between two French towns is 2.5cm.

Whilst making the journey, a signpost says that the destination is 60 kilometres away.

Use the conversion 5 miles = 8 kilometres to calculate how far has already been travelled.

Give your answer in kilometres.

Question 16

A teacher takes a small group of students to a museum in a taxi.

The taxi fare is £2.10 plus an additional 36p per 400m of the journey (or part thereof).

The distance to the museum is 3.7km.

What is the total cost of the journey?

Question 17

A school trip is planned for a total of 20 people in a school minibus. The trip involves driving 70 miles in the UK and 280km in Europe.

The minibus can travel 8km on each litre of petrol, and petrol costs £1.15 per litre.

How much will each person on the trip need to pay to cover the cost of the fuel?

Question 18

A map is drawn to a scale of 1:1,500,000.

On that map, two towns are 18cm apart.

On a journey between those towns, a signpost says that the destination is 60 miles away.

Given that 5 miles = 8 kilometres, how far has already been travelled? Give your answer in miles (to the nearest mile).

Question 19

According to the service book, a minibus can get 25 miles to the gallon.

The petrol tank of the minibus can hold 95 litres of petrol.

On a school trip in Austria, the minibus drives at an average speed of 100km/h.

The petrol tank is filled at 10am, and the group stops for a 45-minute lunch break at 1:15pm.

Use the following conversions to work out what time the minibus will next need to stop for petrol (to the nearest minute).

- 1 Gallon = 4.5 Litres

- 5 Miles = 8 Kilometres

Question 20

A teacher is planning a trip to France that involves a Dover to Calais ferry crossing and a drive from Calais to Paris.

The ferry crossing will take 1 hour, 15 minutes and the drive is a distance of 290km. The teacher expects that the average speed for the drive will be 55 miles per hour.

The group need to arrive at a hostel in Paris by 9pm (UK time).

If ferries leave Dover at 13-minutes past, 33-minutes past and 53-minutes past every hour, what is the latest ferry that the group can get on and still expect to arrive at the hostel on time?

Solutions

Fully worked solutions to all of these questions can be accessed at www.qtsskillstest.com/measurements

Mental Arithmetic Questions

1) 50cm

2) 60 miles

3) 13.2lbs

4) 45cm

5) 169cm^2

6) 2 hours, 20 minutes

7) 1.2km

8) 175ml

9) 80km/hr

10) 250mm

On-Screen Questions

11) £30

12) 43.75 miles per hour

13) 45.68 degrees

14) *30 kilometres per hour*

15) *40km*

16) *£5.70*

17) *£2.82*

18) *109 miles*

19) *7:12pm*

20) *4:13pm*

Ratio

What Ratio Is

In addition to the topics that could come up on any part of the test, there are a few more things that are likely to appear on the on-screen section of the test. One of these things is ratio.

When you work with proportion (fractions, decimals and percentages), you are comparing one part to the whole. For example, if there were 13 boys in a class of 30, you would express this as $^{13}/_{30}$.

With ratio, you compare one part to another part, so in the example above you would compare the number of boys to the number of girls. You separate the two values with a colon, so the ratio of boys to girls would be written as 13:17, meaning that there are 13 boys for every 17 girls.

The order that you write the numbers in the ratio makes a difference. Whichever thing is written first in the question is also written first in the ratio. For example, if the ratio of knives to forks is 4:3 it means you have 4 knives for every 3 forks, not the other way around.

Simplifying Ratios

It is possible to simplify a ratio in a similar way to how you would simplify a fraction. Divide both numbers by the same thing until they are as low as possible. For example, if you have the ratio 8:12, you can divide both numbers by 4 to give you 2:3 as the simplest form of the ratio (if you prefer you could do this step-by-step, and first divide both numbers by 2 to get the ratio 4:6, and then divide by 2 again to get 2:3).

Worked Example

Simplify the ratio 105:45.

You need to find a number that you could divide both 105 and 45 by. There are a few options that you could use, but 5 is probably the easiest one to notice.

105 ÷ 5 = 21 and 45 ÷ 5 = 9 so the ratio is simplified to 21:9.

Now check whether this can be simplified further. It can, because both 21 and 9 can be divided by 3.

21 ÷ 3 = 7 and 9 ÷ 3 = 3 so the ratio is now simplified to 7:3.

This cannot be simplified any further, so the simplest form of the ratio is 7:3.

Answer: 7:3

Scaling Up a Ratio

Ratio is likely to come into play in questions where you need to scale that ratio up to a larger amount. In this case, you need to work out how much you multiply the number in your ratio by to get your given quantity, and then multiply the other number in your ratio by the same amount to get your answer.

Worked Example

The ratio of infants to juniors in a primary school is 3:5. There are 90 infants in the school. How many juniors are there?

The best way to do this is to create a table, and on the top row write the values in the ratio for infants and juniors. On the second row, fill in the value given (in this case 90) in the appropriate column (infants).

Infants	Juniors
3	5
90	

× 30 (infants)   **× 30** (juniors)

Work out what you need to multiply the values on the top row by in order to get the values on the second row as the answer. You can work this out by dividing 90 by 3, and you will find that the answer is 30. Then multiply the value for juniors by 30 to get a final answer of 150.

Answer: 150

Sharing In a Ratio

It is also possible that you will be told the total amount and have to split that amount in a given ratio. For example, a junior school maths class is split between level 4 and level 5 children in the ratio 3:4. If there are 28 children in the class, how many of them are level 5?

In this instance, you use the same method as before, but add an extra column for 'total' and write 28 on the second row of this column.

	Level 4	Level 5	Total
	3	4	7
			28

× 4   × 4

From the final column, it can be seen that each value in the top row must be multiplied by 4 to get the values on the bottom row.

This means there is a total of 3 × 4 = 12 level 4 children and 4 × 4 = 16 level 5 children.

Top Tip

A good way to check your answers for this kind of question is to add them together and see if they make the desired total. In the example above, the answers were 12 and 16. When we add together 12 and 16, the answer is 28, which we know is the total number of children in the class, so this verifies the answers that we have obtained.

Worked Example

In a primary school, the ratio of male teachers to female teachers is 2:11. If there are 26 teachers altogether, how many of them are men?

Start by writing out the ratio, making sure to include a column for 'total'.

	Male	Female	Total
	2	11	13
			26

× 2 ⊂ ⟶　　　　　⟶ ⊃ **× 2**

Use the last column to find what number to multiply the top row by.

26 ÷ 13 = 2, so multiply each of the values by 2.

As the question asks how many teachers are men, the new value for male teachers is 2 × 2 = 4 men.

You can check this by also multiplying the number of women by 2 to get 22 and doing 22 + 4 = 26, so you can be confident that 4 is the correct answer.

Answer: 4

Three (Or More) Part Ratios

You may sometimes encounter a ratio that has three or more numbers in it. The idea with these is exactly the same as when you are just comparing two numbers, and you can simplify, scale up or share in these ratios using the same methods.

For example, if you are told that the favourite flavours of crisps of 30 students are ready salted, cheese & onion, and salt & vinegar in the ratio 1:3:6, it means that for every one student who prefers ready salted, there are three who prefer cheese and onion, and six who prefer salt and vinegar. You can work out how many students like each flavour using a table as before, just adding in another column for the additional number in the ratio.

Ready Salted	Cheese & Onion	Salt & Vinegar	Total
1	3	6	10
			30

× 3 ⊂ ⟶　　　　　⟶ ⊃ **× 3**

You would need to multiply the numbers in the top row by 3, so this would mean there are 3 students who prefer ready salted, 9 who prefer cheese & onion, and 18 who prefer salt & vinegar.

Practice Questions on Ratio

Question 1

In a box of 30 calculators, there are scientific and non-scientific calculators in the ratio 2:3.

A teacher wants to give a class of 22 pupils an exam that requires them to each use a scientific calculator.

How many scientific calculators will he need to borrow from another teacher?

Question 2

In a P.E. lesson, children chose hockey or rugby in a ratio 5:6.

There are 15 children who chose hockey.

How many children are there altogether?

Question 3

Three classes are asked to give their opinions about a potential change to the school day.

Information about the classes is given in the table below.

	Number of Children in Class	Ratio of those who like the new school day to those who like the old school day
Class A	28	5:2
Class B	25	4:1
Class C	27	2:1

Altogether how many children like the new idea for the school day?

Question 4

Five students raise money for charity.

The amounts they raise are £7.10, £5.40, £6.30, £10.50 and £6.10.

The money is divided between 3 charities in the ratio 1:2:3.

How much will each charity get?

Question 5

A teaching assistant splits his time between Charlie and Natasha in the ratio 2:3.

If he is able to work with them for a total of 6 hours in a day, how much of that time does he spend working with Natasha?

Question 6

A maths department divided lessons between number, algebra, shape and data handling in the ratio 3:2:3:1.

Each week there are 3 maths lessons, each lasting 55 minutes.

In hours and minutes, how long is spent studying algebra in a twelve week term?

Question 7

In P.E., a group of boys and girls were given the choice between gymnastics and rounders.

The boys chose in the ratio 1:4.

The girls chose in the ratio 3:1.

Altogether, 16 boys chose rounders.

There were an equal number of boys and girls.

How many people chose gymnastics?

Question 8

In a college, the ratio of students doing vocational qualifications to those doing academic qualifications was 4:7.

There were 141 more people doing academic qualifications than vocational qualifications. How many students were in the college altogether?

Question 9

Eight students raise money by doing a sponsored bike ride.

The money that they raise is split between a school project and a charity in the ratio 3:1.

The money each student raised is shown below.

Student	Money Raised
James	£8.63
Rhea	£6.75
Lisa	£9.31
Jack	£13.21
Ellie	£9.82
Scott	£16.05
David	£5.25
Danielle	£10.70

How much money was donated to charity?

Question 10

A primary school splits year 1 and year 2 students into a stretch group, a core group and a support group in the ratio 2:4:1.

There are 18 children in the stretch group.

How many year 1 and year 2 children are there altogether in the school?

Solutions

Fully worked solutions to all of these questions can be accessed at www.qtsskillstests.com/ratio

On-Screen Questions

1) 10

2) 33

3) 58

4) £5.90, £11.80 & £17.70

5) 3 hours, 36 minutes

6) 7 hours, 20 minutes

7) 19

8) 517

9) £19.93

10) 63

Averages & Range

The Three Averages

Sometimes a question will present you with a large collection of data, either in a list, chart or graph. When this happens, it is often helpful if you have one number that can represent the whole group. This number is called an average.

There are three different types of average that you need to know for the on-screen part of the test.

The first type of average is known as the **MODE**. The mode is the value that appears in the list most often. It can be a number, but it can also be another piece of information. For example, if you were given a list of the grades students achieved in an exam, the most common grade would be the mode.

It is possible that when you are finding the mode, there will be more than one value that is the joint most common. In this circumstance, both values are modes. Mode is the only kind of average that can give you more than one value.

Some questions will use the word 'modal'. This is another way of referring to the mode, often used when speaking of groups.

The second type of average is the **MEDIAN**. This is the middle value. To find it you need to start by arranging the data you have been given from smallest to largest (sometimes this will already be done for you). Once you have done this, eliminate the highest and lowest values. Keep eliminating the highest and lowest remaining values until you just have the middle value remaining. This will be the median.

When you are asked to find the median, a common mistake is to find the middle value without first putting the numbers in order. Remember that the numbers must be lined up before you can work out what the median is.

Sometimes, when you need the median you are left with two middle numbers, not one. For example, consider this list of numbers: 2, 3, 4, 6, 8, 9. The numbers are already in order, so we can eliminate the top and bottom values: ~~2~~, 3, 4, 6, 8, ~~9~~. Then repeat this ~~2, 3~~, 4, 6, ~~8, 9~~ and the 4 and 6 both remain. In this case, the value half way between them is the median, so halfway between 4 and 6 is 5. (A useful trick for working this out is adding the numbers together and dividing the answer by 2).

Finally, there is the **MEAN**. To work out the mean, add all of the values together and divide your answer by how many values there are.

Worked Example

A group of 11 students took a spelling test. Their scores are recorded below.

7, 6, 9, 4, 6, 8, 7, 6, 10, 5, 8

Find: (a) the mode; (b) the median; (c) the mean of these numbers.

To find the mode, see which score appears most frequently in the list.

6 appears three times (which is more than any other number) so the mode is 6.

For the median, arrange the numbers in order from the smallest to the largest.

4, 5, 6, 6, 6, 7, 7, 8, 8, 9, 10.

Now eliminate numbers from the top and bottom of the list until you are left with just one number in the middle of the list.

4, 5, 6, 6, 6, 7, 7, 8, 8, 9, 10

The median is 7.

To work out the mean, add together all the numbers in the list.

4 + 5 + 6 + 6 + 6 + 7 + 7 + 8 + 8 + 9 + 10 = 76.

Divide this answer by how many numbers there are.

76 ÷ 11 = 6.9

The mean is 6.9 (to 1 decimal place).

Answer: (a) 6; (b) 7; (c) 6.9

Top Tip

When you work out an average, it should look the right size to represent a typical value from your list. In the above example, the averages were 6, 7 and 6.9, which are all of the right kind of size for a list of numbers where the lowest value is 4 and the highest value is 10. Had one of the averages worked out to be 2397 or 0.001, then this would be an indication that something had gone wrong in one of the calculations.

Range

It is also possible that you will be asked a question about range. Range doesn't represent the data like an average does, but it shows you how spread out the data is. If the range is low, it means all the values are close together. If the range is high it means the data is more spread out.

To calculate the range, subtract the lowest value in the list from the highest value in the list.

Worked Example

A group of 11 students took a spelling test. Their scores are recorded below.

7, 6, 9, 4, 6, 8, 7, 6, 10, 5, 8

Find the range.

The highest value on this list is 10 and the lowest value is 4.

To find the range, subtract the lowest value from the highest value.

10 - 4 = 6

Answer: 6

Sometimes you can use the range and one of the averages to work out whether a value is possibly on your list. The key point to remember is that no two values can differ by more than the range.

For example, you may be told that the median test score of a class is 25 and the range is 15 and be asked whether it is possible that somebody in the group scored less than 10.

If somebody did score less than ten (for example nine), then the difference between their score and the median would be 25 – 9 = 16, which is more than the range, so this is impossible. You can, therefore, conclude that nobody scored less than ten – and by similar logic can conclude that nobody scored more than 40.

Worked Example

A teacher produced the following table to show the marks achieved in an end of term science test by pupils in three year nine classes.

	Marks (Percentage)		
	Range	Median	Mode
Class A	35	48	55
Class B	48	30	52
Class C	70	55	60

Tick all true statements:

- **No pupils in Class A achieved less that 20%.**

- **At least one pupil in Class B achieved more than 78%**

- **All pupils in Class C achieved at least 35%**

To answer this question, consider each statement in turn.

*If the first statement were true, then nobody could have scored less than 20% (for example 19%). Compare the difference between this score and the mode (because for this class, the difference from 19% to the mode will be greater than the difference from 19% to the median). 55 – 19 = 36, which is greater than the range so it is impossible that a pupil scored less than 20% and the statement is **true**.*

If the second statement were true, then somebody scored more than 78% (for example 79%). Compare the difference between this score and the median (because this time it is the median that will give the greater difference). 79 – 30 = 49, which is greater than the range so it is impossible that a pupil scored more than 78% and the statement is **false.**

The third statement uses a slightly different thought process. If the statement is true then the lowest score will be 35% (or higher). Because the range is 70, the highest score would be 70 percentage points higher than 35%, which would be 105%, but this is impossible as a percentage score is out of 100. Therefore the statement is **false***.*

Answer: True, False, False

Averages From Tables

Some questions on averages and range do not present the data in a list but give you the data in a grouped table.

A grouped table shows you how many times each value occurs. To find the averages, you need to extract the data and then use the principles outlined.

To find range, look at the lowest and highest values on the table (not frequencies) and subtract them (make sure that the frequency is not zero for these values).

To find the mode, look for the value that has the greatest frequency.

To find the median, add up the total frequency and find the frequency that is halfway through the total. Then count along the frequencies until you see which value this halfway frequency corresponds to. This value is the median.

To find the mean, multiply each value by the number of times it occurs (the frequency) and add all of these values together. Then divide the answer by the total frequency.

Worked Example

A form tutor produced a table to show how many days each pupil in a class of 30 was absent in a term.

Days Absent	0	1	2	3	4
Number of Pupils	9	7	6	6	2

Find (a) the range; (b) the mode; (c) the median; and (d) the mean.

To find the range, use the first row of the table. You need to subtract the lowest number of days off from the highest number of days off (making sure that the number of pupils for that amount of days is not 0). The lowest number is 0 and the highest is 4, so the range is 4 – 0 = 4.

For the mode, you want the amount of days off that occurs most often (i.e. has the highest number of pupils). There are 9 pupils who have 0 days off, which is higher than any other amount of days off, so the mode is 0.

For the median, you need to find the 'half-way' person. Because there are 30 people altogether, there will be two middle people (this always happens if it is an even number of people) and these will be the 15th and 16th people. You then need to count off people. The first 9 had 0 days absent and the next 7 had 1. This makes a total of 16, so both the 15th and 16th people had 1 day absent, giving a median of 1.

To work out the mean, you need to add up the number of days off for every pupil.

9 pupils had 0 days off so this gives (9 × 0).

7 pupils had 1 day off, giving (7 × 1).

Do the same for the other columns to get (2 × 6), (3 × 6), and (4 × 2).

Work out these values and then add the answers together.

0 + 7 + 12 + 18 + 8 = 45. Divide this total by the number of pupils there are in the class.

45 ÷ 30 gives a mean of 1.5.

Answer: (a) 4; (b) 0; (c) 1; (d) 1.5

It is also possible that you will be asked to calculate averages from different types of graphs or chart. The techniques for doing this will be outlined in the chapters on the relevant graphs.

Practice Questions on Averages & Range

Question 1

Eight children grew sunflowers and measured them.

The results were 19cm, 14cm, 35cm, 29cm, 18cm, 11cm, 23cm and 26cm.

What was the median height?

Question 2

A group of year 4 students were asked how many books they had read in the last week.

Their answers are in the table below.

Number of Books	0	1	2	3	4
Number of Children	7	19	14	4	1

What is the mean number of books read by this group?

Question 3

A group of year 4 students were asked how many books they had read in the last week.

Their answers are in the table below.

Number of Books	0	1	2	3	4
Number of Children	7	19	14	4	1

What is the median number of books read by this group?

Question 4

This table show the KS2 Science levels across 4 schools.

	Level 2	Level 3	Level 4	Level 5	Level 6
School A	4	16	19	15	3
School B	7	22	18	13	0
School C	5	19	16	15	2
School D	2	13	21	26	8

What is the modal level across all 4 schools?

Question 5

Five pupils took a spelling test.

The median score was 7.

The mode was 6.

The range was 3.

What was the mean?

Question 6

The levels achieved in English by a group of year 6 students are shown below:

Level	Number of Students
2	2
3	12
4	17
5	20
6	14

What was the median level?

Question 7

Woodside School records the number of GCSE A*-C grades achieved by 150 Year 11 students.

Number of A*-C Grades	Number of Students
0	3
1	6
2	10
3	13
4	19
5	24
6	28
7	18
8	15
9	11
10	3

What was the mean number of A*-C grades?

Question 8

A school records the levels three classes of students achieved at the end of Key Stage 2 in English.

	Level 2	Level 3	Level 4	Level 5	Level 6
Class A	2	9	13	6	0
Class B	1	6	10	9	4
Class C	0	2	12	10	6

Indicate all true statements:

- The modal level is the same for all three classes.

- The range of levels is the same for all three classes.

- The median level is the same for all three classes.

Question 9

A teacher produced the following table to show the marks achieved in an end of term history test by pupils in three year eight classes.

Marks (Out of 50)			
	Range	Median	Mode
Class A	20	30	28
Class B	18	35	25
Class C	35	22	30

Tick all true statements:

- At least one pupil in Class A got full marks.

- No pupils in Class B got less than 15 marks.

- All pupils in Class C scored at least 40%.

Question 10

This table shows the actual age and reading age of 10 children and the value of the reading age minus actual age (in months) has been filled in for the first three students

	Actual Age	**Reading Age**	**Reading Age – Actual Age**
Student A	*10 years, 8 months*	*12 years, 4 months*	*20*
Student B	*10 years, 10 months*	*10 years, 3 months*	*-7*
Student C	*11 years, 0 months*	*10 years, 2 months*	*-10*
Student D	*10 years, 9 months*	*11 years, 3 months*	
Student E	*11 years, 4 months*	*11 years, 4 months*	
Student F	*11 years, 3 months*	*11 years, 11 months*	
Student G	*10 years, 7 months*	*12 years, 1 month*	
Student H	*11 years, 2 months*	*11 years, 0 months*	
Student I	*10 years, 6 months*	*10 years, 10 months*	
Student J	*10 years, 9 months*	*11 years, 0 months*	

What was the mean value in months of the reading age minus actual age?

Solutions

Fully worked solutions to all of these questions can be accessed at www.qtsskillstests.com/averages

On-Screen Questions

1) 21cm

2) 1.4

3) 1

4) Level 4

5) 7.2

6) Level 5

7) 5.36

8) True, False, False

9) False, True, False

10) 4 months

Formulae

Worded Formulae

Some of the questions in the on-screen section require you to use formulae.

A formula is a set of instructions that shows you the relationship between two or more things and can be written using words or using symbols.

An example of a formula that is given using words would be converting from degrees Celsius to degrees Fahrenheit.

To find the number of degrees Fahrenheit, multiply the number of degrees Celsius by 1.8, then add 32 to the answer

To use a worded formula, simply follow the instructions for the number that you have been given.

Worked Example

Use the worded formula below to convert 20° Celsius into degrees Fahrenheit.

To find the number of degrees Fahrenheit, multiply the number of degrees Celsius by 1.8, then add 32 to the answer

The first instruction given is to multiply the number of degrees Celsius by 1.8.

20 × 1.8 = 36.

The next step is to add 32 to your answer.

36 + 32 = 68.

Answer: 68° Fahrenheit

Working Backwards

It is also possible to use a formula to work backwards from the final answer to original value. To do this, carry out the steps in the reverse order and do the opposite of what the formula says (for example, add instead of subtract, multiply instead of divide).

Worked Example

Use the worded formula below to convert 122° Fahrenheit into degrees Celsius.

To find the number of degrees Fahrenheit, multiply the number of degrees Celsius by 1.8, then add 32 to the answer

Because you need to work backwards, start with the last instruction in the formula, which is 'add 32'. You need to do the opposite of this, so subtract 32.

122 – 32 = 90.

The next step is to multiply by 1.8. The opposite of this is to divide by 1.8.

90 ÷ 1.8 = 50

Answer: 50° Celsius

Note – To check this answer you could put 50° into the original formula and see if the answer comes out as 122°.

Writing Formulae With Symbols

Often you will see formulae written using symbols rather than words.

For example, the formula that was used in the example above to convert temperatures from degrees Celsius to degrees Fahrenheit could be written as:

$$F = 1.8C + 32$$

Although the formula can appear more intimidating when it is written in this form, it is exactly the same as the worded version (only shorter). The 'F' and 'C' stand for the temperature in Fahrenheit and

Celsius respectively, and instead of writing out the words 'multiply' and 'add' we have exchanged them for mathematical symbols (where the formula has a number and a letter together – or two letters – you need to multiply them, so 1.8C means 1.8 lots of C, or 1.8 × C).

To use the formula, put the value that you know for degrees Celsius in place of the C, so to convert 20° Celsius into degrees Fahrenheit your calculation would be 1.8 × 20 = 36 + 32 = 68°, as before (and again, you could make these steps in reverse if you knew 'F' and wanted to find 'C').

Sometimes a formula may have room for you to add in more than one value. For example you may find the total cost (£T) of a group of A adults and C children using the formula T = 5A + 3C. In this case you would need to insert both the number of adults and the number of children into the formula.

When you are working with formulae, you need to be careful with units. If you read the question thoroughly you should be told what units you are working in. For example, in the formula above, the total cost is £T, so when you find T you know that it will be in pounds, rather than pence or euros or anything else.

It is also important to remember that there is a correct order to perform the calculations in your formula, and it does make a difference if you get the order wrong.

- Do anything in brackets first.

- Then do any divisions or multiplications.

- Lastly do any additions or subtractions.

For example, if you had to work out 5 + 4 × 3 in your formula, you would do the multiplication first. 4 × 3 = 12, leaving 5 + 12 = 17. Had you done the calculations in the wrong order, you would have got an answer of 27 instead.

Top Tip

When you have a formula, make sure you know what each symbol stands for (this is not necessarily the first letter of what the symbol represents). It can be a good idea when you have a formula in symbols to try to write out the same formula in words to make sure you understand what everything symbolises.

Worked Example

The cost (£C) of a school trip for n pupils can be worked out using the following formula:

$$C = 7n + 80$$

What is the total cost if 52 pupils go on the trip?

The first step is to be clear what everything in the formula stands for. We are told in the question that C represents the cost and that n pupils are going, so n must be the number of pupils.

As we have 52 pupils going on the trip, we work out the cost by putting 52 into the formula instead of n.

52 × 7 + 80 = 444

Answer: £444

Practice Questions on Formulae

Question 1

Students taking Geography sit two exams and submit a piece of coursework.

The final mark is calculated by adding together the score on the two exams, dividing the result by two and then adding on the coursework score.

If a student scored 37 on exam 1, 49 on exam 2 and 28 on the coursework, what was her final mark?

Question 2

Students complete 3 English modules and work out their overall score (S) using the following formula (where A, B and C represent the scores in modules A, B and C respectively):

$$S = (2A + B + C) \div 4$$

If a student scores 76 on module A, 63 on module B and 81 on module C, what was his overall score?

Question 3

The cost in pounds of a prom for school leavers is worked out using the following formula:

Cost = £140 + £17 × number of people attending

How much would the prom cost if 112 students and 24 staff members attend?

Question 4

A teacher needs to order new stationary supplies for her class.

The total cost in pence (C) of r rulers and p boxes of pencils (each containing 10 pencils) is worked out with this formula:

C = 14r + 80p

If she wants 75 rulers and 75 pencils, how much will she have to pay?

Give your answer in pounds and pence.

Question 5

In a junior school fundraiser, the total raised (in pounds) is worked out using the following formula:

Total Raised = 1.5w + 1.8x + 2y + 2.6z

Where w, x, y and z are the numbers of children in years 3, 4, 5 and 6 respectively.

A junior school has the following year sizes:

	Year 3	Year 4	Year 5	Year 6
Number of Children	41	37	46	35

How much money will they raise?

Question 6

The each-way cost (£C) of hiring a coach for a school trip of m miles is found by the following formula:

$$C = 85 + 1.30m$$

A teacher has £150 each way to spend on the coach.

What is the furthest distance that the trip can be?

Question 7

A student's overall mark (M) in science is obtained from their exam score (E), coursework score (C) and practical score (P) using the following formula:

$$M = 0.5E + 0.3C + 0.2P$$

The scores achieved by three students are shown on the table below:

	Exam	Coursework	Practical
Amy	40	90	85
Bryony	65	70	60
Calum	75	60	55

What was the highest overall mark achieved?

Question 8

The overall marks (M) achieved in a science qualification are worked out by combining the coursework marks (C) and the exam marks (E) according to the following formula.

$$M = (3C + E) \div 4$$

Jason scored 58 on his coursework.

To achieve the grade he desires, he needs a total score of 60 or above.

What is the minimum mark that he can score on the exam to achieve this?

Question 9

Temperature is converted from Celsius (C) to Fahrenheit (F) using the following formula.

$$F = 1.8C + 32$$

A teacher plans to take a group of students outside to perform an investigation, but is advised not to do so if the temperature is higher than 80°F or lower than 35°F.

The weather forecast predicts the following temperatures for the upcoming week:

Monday	0°C
Tuesday	4°C
Wednesday	-1°C
Thursday	2°C
Friday	1°C

On which days is the teacher able to take the children outside?

Question 10

A teacher is organising a school camping trip.

The total cost is calculated using the following formula.

Cost = £150 + (number of students × £25)

If the school charges students £30 to attend, how many students will need to attend in order for the trip to break even?

Solutions

Fully worked solutions to all of these questions can be accessed at www.qtsskillstests.com/formulae

On-Screen Questions

1) 71

2) 74

3) £2452

4) £16.90

5) £311.10

6) 50 miles

7) 00.5

8) 66

9) Tuesday & Thursday

10) 30

Weighting

Weighting by a Formula

There is a particular type of question which often comes up on the on-screen tests, where you will have to work out a final score from several different components - possibly exams and coursework, or different modules of work.

The difficulty usually comes in the fact that the components do not all carry the same value, so it is not simply a case of adding up the individual scores, or even of finding an average of them.

Usually, the 'weighting' will be expressed in one of two ways. It is possible that you will be given a formula to put the individual scores into. In this case, you may wish to refer to the previous chapter on formulae as all of the same principles apply.

Worked Example

A course is assessed by a written exam and a piece of coursework. The total mark (T) that a student obtains is worked out according to the following formula, where W is the percentage score in the written exam and C is the percentage score in the coursework.

$$T = 0.7W + 0.3C$$

What was the overall weighted score of a student who scored 72% on the written exam and 54% on the coursework?

Put the scores given into the formula.

T = 0.7 × 72% + 0.3 × 54%

T = 50.4% + 16.2% = 66.6%

Answer: 66.6%

Be careful when the formula asks for the percentage score (such as the formula above). When the question states the score as a percentage then you can put it straight into the formula (as in the worked example), but when you are given the number of marks you will need to first convert it into a percentage and then put it into the formula.

Worked Example

A course is assessed by a written exam and a piece of coursework. The total mark (T) that a student obtains is worked out according to the following formula, where W is the percentage score in the written exam and C is the percentage score in the coursework.

$$T = 0.7W + 0.3C$$

What was the overall weighted score of a student who scored 27 out of 60 on the written exam and 22 out of 40 on the coursework?

First turn the scores into percentages.

For the written exam, 27 ÷ 60 = 0.45 × 100 = 45%.

For the coursework, 22 ÷ 40 = 0.55 × 100 = 55%

Put the scores given into the formula.

T = 0.7 × 45% + 0.3 × 55%

T = 31.5% + 16.5% = 48%

Answer: 48%

Weighting by Proportion

The other possibility is that you will be told the proportion of the overall mark that each component is worth. For example, if in an exam, paper A is worth 25% of the total and paper B is worth 75% of the total, you would work out the number of marks scored on paper A out of the total as a fraction and multiply this by 25%. Do the same for paper B, only this time multiply by 75%. Then add together the scores for both papers to get the final score.

When you are given the proportion of the overall weighting for each component, it will not necessarily be in the form of a percentage. You could be given a fraction, a decimal or even a ratio. The best way to approach such a question would be to convert the proportions you have been given into percentages and then answer the question in the way outlined above for percentages.

Top Tip

The best way to approach weighting as proportion questions is to think of them as a series of smaller percentages questions. This is much less overwhelming than approaching the whole question, and once you have done it you can simply add your answers together.

Worked Example

A science test is made up of 3 papers. The first 2 papers each have a maximum of 40 marks, and the third paper has a maximum of 60 marks.

The weighting of the 3 papers is given below:

Paper 1	Paper 2	Paper 3
20%	30%	50%

What is the final weighted mark (as a percentage) of a student who scored 24 on paper 1, 28 on paper 2 and 42 on paper 3?

For each paper work out the fraction of the total number of marks scored and multiply by the weighted percentage.

On paper 1, the fraction is $^{24}/_{40}$.

Work out $24 \div 40 \times 20\% = 12\%$.

On paper 2, the fraction is $^{28}/_{40}$.

Work out $28 \div 40 \times 30\% = 21\%$

On paper 3, the fraction is $^{42}/_{60}$.

Work out 42 ÷ 60 × 50% = 35%

The total score is the answer when these weighted percentages are added together.

12% + 21% + 35% = 68%.

Answer: 68%

Practice Questions on Weighting

Question 1

The scores for an exam (E) and coursework (C) in history are weighted according to the following formula.

Total Mark = (1.5C + 2.5E) ÷ 4

What is the total mark for a student who scored 52 on the coursework and 76 on the exam?

Question 2

An R.E. exam is made up of 3 modules.

Module 1 is weighted at 15%, module 2 is weighted at 40% and module 3 is weighted at 45%.

The scores of a student in those 3 modules are displayed below.

	Module 1	**Module 2**	**Module 3**
Marks Achieved	12	17	38
Total Marks Available	30	45	60

What is their overall percentage score in the exam?

Give your answer to 1 decimal place.

Question 3

A maths exam is made up of 2 papers.

Paper 1 counts for $^2/_5$ of the total mark and paper 2 counts for the rest.

A student scores 41 out of 60 on paper 1 and 69 out of 80 on paper 2.

The grade boundaries for the exam are displayed below:

A*	A	B	C	D	E	F	G
84%	76%	67%	60%	53%	44%	35%	26%

What grade did the student get?

Question 4

A student takes 5 exams: V, W, X, Y & Z.

The overall weighted score is calculated according to the following formula:

$$\textbf{Total Score = 20 x } [\frac{V}{40} + \frac{W}{75} + \frac{X}{60} + \frac{Y}{80} + \frac{Z}{50}]$$

If a student scores 26, 56, 39, 55 and 41 respectively on exams V, W, X, Y and Z, what is her total score? (Give your answer to the nearest whole number)

Question 5

Three pieces of coursework are weighted in the ratio 1:3:4.

All three exams are out of 30 marks and a student scored 20 on the first piece, 25 on the second piece and 18 on the third piece.

What is their overall weighted score?

Give your answer to one decimal place.

Question 6

A business studies course is graded according to the following weighting:

Coursework	Final Exam
35%	65%

The coursework is marked out of 40, and the final exam out of 120.

What is the final weighted percentage score of a student who scored 18 on the coursework and 99 on the final exam?

Question 7

The sections of an exam paper are weighted in the ratio 1:3:6.

What is the overall weighted percentage score of a student who scored as below:

	Marks Scored	Marks Available
Section 1	13	20
Section 2	32	40
Section 3	35	75

Question 8

A Physics exam is made of three sections.

The first two sections each have a maximum score of 50 marks and the third section has a maximum score of 80 marks.

The weighting of the three sections is given below:

Section 1	Section 2	Section 3
20%	30%	50%

One student scored 28 marks on paper 1, 34 marks on paper 2, and 66 marks on paper 3.

What was the student's final weighted percentage score?

Question 9

The overall score for a history course is found from the percentage coursework score (C) and the percentage exam score (E), weighted according to the following formula.

Total Score = [2C + 3E] ÷ 5

What was the overall weighted score of a student who scored 32 out of 50 on the coursework and 93 out of 120 on the exam?

Question 10

In a French course, the speaking element is weighted at 0.2, the reading element is weighted at 0.2, the writing element is weighted at 0.3 and the listening element is weighted at 0.3

What is the overall weighted percentage score of the student with the following marks?

Section	Total Marks Available	Marks Scored
Speaking	20	16
Reading	75	51
Writing	80	68
Listening	100	59

Solutions

Fully worked solutions to all of these questions can be accessed at www.qtsskillstests.com/weighting

On-Screen Questions

1) 67

2) 49.6%

3) Grade A

4) 71

5) 69.6%

6) 69.375%

7) 58.5%

8) 72.85%

9) 72.1%

10) 72.8%

Tables

Reading a Table

A substantial part of the on-screen section of the QTS numeracy test is about interpreting data from various tables, charts or graphs, and the next few chapters of the book will explore the different ways that this data may be presented.

The first type of data to become confident with is data that is presented in a table. The idea of a table is that each row (or column) represents a different category, and shows a numerical value for that category.

For example, a primary school may produce a table to show how many children are in each year group. To do this, each row of the table could represent a different year group, with the year group being written in the first column (the row header) and the number of children in that year group written in the second column.

Year Group	Number of Children
Reception	24
Year 1	29
Year 2	28
Year 3	31
Year 4	30
Year 5	26
Year 6	28
Total	196

The very top row of this table shows the headers for each column so you can see what the data represents. The next row says 'Reception' in the column for 'Year Group' and '24' in the column for number of children, which tells you that there are 24 children in the reception group. The next row tells you that there are 29 children in Year 1, and so on.

It is also possible that the same data could be represented in a table with each year group being represented by a column. You would read this table in exactly the same way, using the row and column headers as the guide for what the value in each cell represents.

Year Group	Reception	Year 1	Year 2	Year 3	Year 4	Year 5	Year 6	Total
Number of Children	24	29	28	31	30	26	28	196

Worked Example

A primary school produces a table to show the number of children in each year group.

Year Group	Reception	Year 1	Year 2	Year 3	Year 4	Year 5	Year 6	Total
Number of Children	24	29	28	31	30	26	28	196

Which two year groups contain the same number of children?

You need to look for the two values on the 'number of children' row that are the same.

There are two occurrences of the number 28, one of them in the 'Year 2' column and the other in the 'Year 6' column.

This means that both Year 2 and Year 6 contain 28 children.

Answer: Year 2 and Year 6

Two-Way Tables

Many tables that you encounter will categorise data in more than one way. For example, the table considered above may be expanded so that not only does each row represent a different year group, but also each column represents a different school.

Year Group	Riverside School	Hillside School	Beachside School	Total
Reception	24	27	25	76
Year 1	29	30	26	85
Year 2	28	26	31	85
Year 3	31	27	28	86
Year 4	30	30	28	88
Year 5	26	29	29	84
Year 6	28	27	30	85
Total	196	196	197	589

In this case, the '24' on the second row indicates that there are 24 children in the reception group (because the row that it is on has 'reception' as the header) at Riverside School (because it is the column that has 'Riverside School' as the column header). Similarly, there are 27 children in the reception group at Hillside School and 25 children in the reception group at Beachside School.

Top Tip

When you have a two-way table, the total that is given at the end of a row or the bottom of a column is just the total for the category that is represented by the row or column in question. For example, in the table above, the '76' that is in the total column for the 'Reception' row is the total number of children in the reception year across all three schools. Similarly, the '196' at the bottom of the 'Riverside School' column is the total of all the children at Riverside School across all the years. The very bottom right cell (589) is the 'total total' and this is the number of students altogether in all of the schools in any year.

Worked Example

The table below shows the number of children in each year group in three primary schools.

Year Group	Riverside School	Hillside School	Beachside School	Total
Reception	24	27	25	76
Year 1	29	30	26	85
Year 2	28	26	31	85
Year 3	31	27	28	86
Year 4	30	30	28	88
Year 5	26	29	29	84
Year 6	28	27	30	85
Total	196	196	197	589

The Local Education Authority recommends that all classes be made up of less than thirty children.

What percentage of the children are in classes of thirty or more? Give your answer as a percentage to 1 decimal place.

First identify the classes that are made up of 30 or more children.

There are the Year 3 and Year 4 classes at Riverside School, the Year 1 and Year 4 classes at Hillside School and the Year 2 and Year 6 classes at Beachside School.

Add up the total number of children in these classes.

31 + 30 + 30 + 30 + 31 + 30 = 182

There are 589 children altogether, so work out what 182 is as a percentage of 589.

182 ÷ 589 = 0.309 × 100 = 30.9%

Answer: 30.9%

Double Headed Tables

Sometimes a table may need to categorise data in three (or even four) ways. One of the ways of doing this is by including sub-headers within the main header for each column or each row (or both).

For example, the table below takes the same data that is shown in the table in the section above, but also shows the breakdown of girls and boys within each year group at each school.

Year Group	Riverside School		Hillside School		Beachside School		Total
	Boys	Girls	Boys	Girls	Boys	Girls	
Reception	13	11	12	15	11	14	76
Year 1	16	13	16	14	14	12	85
Year 2	11	17	13	13	14	17	85
Year 3	15	16	15	12	12	16	86
Year 4	16	14	14	16	15	13	88
Year 5	15	11	16	13	18	11	84
Year 6	13	15	14	13	14	16	85
Total	99	97	100	96	98	99	589

The first two cells in the 'Reception' row (after the row header) show 13 and 11. Both of these are under the overall column header of 'Riverside School', but the 13 is under the sub-header 'boys' and the 11 is under the sub-header 'girls'. This means that there are 13 boys and 11 girls in the reception class at Riverside School.

Worked Example

The table below shows the number of children in each year group in three primary schools.

Year Group	Riverside School		Hillside School		Beachside School		
	Boys	Girls	Boys	Girls	Boys	Girls	Total
Reception	13	11	12	15	11	14	76
Year 1	16	13	16	14	14	12	85
Year 2	11	17	13	13	14	17	85
Year 3	15	16	15	12	12	16	86
Year 4	16	14	14	16	15	13	88
Year 5	15	11	16	13	18	11	84
Year 6	13	15	14	13	14	16	85
Total	99	97	100	96	98	99	589

Indicate all true statements.

- **There were more girls than boys in Year 3 across all three schools.**

- **All three schools had a greater number of boys than girls.**

- **More than half of all classes had a greater number of boys than girls.**

Consider each statement in turn.

For the first statement, add together the number of girls in Year 3 and then add the number of boys in Year 3.

Girls: 16 + 12 + 16 = 44

Boys: 15 + 15 + 12 = 42

*The number of girls is higher than the number of boys, so the statement is **true**.*

For the second statement, compare the totals at the bottom of the columns.

For Riverside School, the number of boys is 99 and the number of girls is 97, so the number of boys is higher than the number of girls.

For Hillside School, the number of boys is 100 and the number of girls is 96, so the number of boys is higher than the number of girls.

For Riverside School, the number of boys is 98 and the number of girls is 99, so the number of girls is higher than the number of boys.

*The number of boys is not higher in all three schools, so the statement is **false.***

For the third statement, count up the number of classes where the number of boys is higher than the number of girls.

There are 11 such classes (Riverside School – Reception, Year 1, Year 4, Year 5; Hillside School – Year 1, Year 3, Year 5, Year 6; Beachside School – Year 1, Year 4, Year 5).

*The number of classes altogether is 21. Half of this would be 10.5, so 11 is greater than half and the statement is **true**.*

Answer: True, False, True

Multiple Tables

Sometimes you may be presented with data in more than one table, and you may need to perform calculations from the data in one table to then read the other table.

For example, the first table below shows how grades are assigned to a piece of coursework based on the total score from the three questions and whether the work was submitted on time. The second table shows the scores obtained by five pupils.

Score	91-100	81-90	71-80	61-70	51-60	41-50	31-40	21-30	11-20	0-10
Submitted on time	A	A	A	B	C	D	E	U	U	U
1-7 days late	A	A	B	C	D	E	U	U	U	U
More than 7 days late	A	B	C	D	E	U	U	U	U	U

Name	Submitted	Question 1	Question 2	Question 3
Amelia	*5 days late*	*35*	*21*	*17*
Byron	*On time*	*23*	*18*	*14*
Chris	*On time*	*33*	*25*	*16*
Daisy	*10 days late*	*41*	*28*	*20*
Enrique	*1 day late*	*27*	*19*	*16*

To work out Amelia's overall grade, start by adding together the number of marks she got on the three questions (from the second table).

35 + 21 + 17 = 73.

Now look at the top table and read off the value for someone with 73 marks who submitted the work 5 days late (you will need to use the 71-80 column and the 1-7 days late row). This shows that Amelia's grade was B.

Worked Example

The first table below shows the grade that students receive for a piece of coursework based on their score on three questions and when they submitted the work. The second table shows the scores obtained by five students.

Score	91-100	81-90	71-80	61-70	51-60	41-50	31-40	21-30	11-20	0-10
Submitted on time	A	A	A	B	C	D	E	U	U	U
1-7 days late	A	A	B	C	D	E	U	U	U	U
More than 7 days late	A	B	C	D	E	U	U	U	U	U

Name	Submitted	Question 1	Question 2	Question 3
Amelia	*5 days late*	*35*	*21*	*17*
Byron	*On time*	*23*	*18*	*14*
Chris	*On time*	*33*	*25*	*16*
Daisy	*10 days late*	*41*	*28*	*20*
Enrique	*1 day late*	*27*	*19*	*16*

Which student scored the highest grade?

Work out the grade for each student in turn.

Amelia's total score was 35 + 21 + 17 = 73 and she submitted the work 5 days late. Read this off on the first table to see that her grade was B.

Byron's total score was 23 + 18 + 14 = 55 and he submitted the work on time. Read this off on the first table to see that his grade was C.

Chris's total score was 33 + 25 + 16 = 74 and he submitted the work on time. Read this off on the first table to see that his grade was A.

Daisy's total score was 41 + 28 + 20 = 89 and she submitted the work 10 days late. Read this off on the first table to see that her grade was B.

Enrique's total score was 27 + 19 + 16 = 62 and he submitted the work 1 day late. Read this off on the first table to see that his grade was C.

The person with the highest grade was Chris with grade A.

Answer: Chris

Trends

Sometimes you may be asked about trends from tables.

There are two types of trend that you need to be aware of:

- **Continual trends** – A continual increase is where each value in a category on the table is higher than the previous one (similarly, a continual decrease is where each value in the category is lower than the previous one).

- **Consistent trends** – A consistent increase doesn't just require each score to be higher than the previous score, but it needs the improvement to be exactly the same each time (for example, each value could be exactly 3 higher than the previous value).

Worked Example

A Maths department keeps track of the scores of some students in four practice GCSE exams.

Student	Test 1	Test 2	Test 3	Test 4
Student A	55	59	60	66
Student B	66	71	71	73
Student C	45	47	49	47
Student D	70	72	74	79
Student E	63	68	73	78

(a) Which students showed a continual improvement?

(b) Which students showed a consistent improvement?

Look at the trend for each student in turn.

Student A started by improving from 55 to 59, which is an improvement of four. Then they improved from 59 to 60, which is an improvement of one. Finally, they improved from 60 to 66, which is an improvement of six.

*Student A improved each time, but not by the same amount, so this is **continual** improvement, but not consistent improvement.*

Student B started by improving from 66 to 71, which is an improvement of five. However, they didn't improve from Test 2 to Test 3, so this is neither continual improvement nor consistent improvement.

Student C started by improving from 45 to 47, which is an improvement of two. Then they improved from 47 to 49, which is also an improvement of two. However, from Test 3 to Test 4 their score declined, so this is neither continual improvement nor consistent improvement.

Student D started by improving from 70 to 72, which is an improvement of two. Then they improved from 72 to 74, which is also an improvement of two. Finally, they improved from 74 to 79, which is an improvement of five.

*Student D improved each time, but not by the same amount, so this is **continual** improvement, but not consistent improvement.*

Student E started by improving from 63 to 68, which is an improvement of five. Then they improved from 68 to 73, which is also an improvement of five. Finally, they improved from 73 to 78, which again is an improvement of five.

*Student E improved each time, by exactly the same amount, so this is **continual** improvement and **consistent** improvement.*

Answer: (a) Students A, D & E; (b) Student E

Practice Questions on Tables

Question 1

An attendance officer created the following table to show how many children were absent from school one Monday.

Class	Total Number of Children	Number of Children Absent
A	28	3
B	29	1
C	30	2
D	29	0
E	26	1
F	31	4
G	30	2
H	27	3

What percentage of pupils was absent?

Give your answer to the nearest whole number.

Question 2

A Maths teacher created a table to compare the average percentage score of three classes on the calculator and non-calculator assessments for the three modules that make up their course.

Module	Average Percentage Score		
	Class X	Class Y	Class Z
Module A (Calculator)	55	58	70
Module A (Non-Calculator)	58	63	66
Module B (Calculator)	57	60	74
Module B (Non-Calculator)	61	62	74
Module C (Calculator)	62	68	77
Module C (Non-Calculator)	59	71	78

Indicate all true statements:

- All three classes had a trend of continual improvement on both papers.

- In class Y, the average percentage score was higher for the Non-Calculator paper than for the Calculator paper on all three modules.

- The average score in class Z was higher than the other classes on all six papers.

Question 3

A primary school teacher organises a sponsored run. Ten children take part in the run.

The teacher records the number of laps of the track that each child runs and the amount of money the child raises.

Child	A	B	C	D	E	F	G	H	I	J
Number of Laps	6	10	9	10	7	12	8	11	8	6
Amount Raised	£8.55	£10.08	£8.41	£13.72	£10.60	£16.42	£12.92	£14.15	£7.25	£8.33

Which child raised the most money per lap?

Question 4

The percentages of pupils achieving level 4 or above in English at the end of Key Stage 2 over a six-year period at an Academy chain are shown in the table.

School	2012	2013	2014	2015	2016	2017
A	41.6	41.9	42.4	42.5	43.1	43.6
B	37.1	37.3	37.3	37.5	37.9	38.4
C	40.6	41.2	41.8	42.4	43.0	43.6
D	47.0	46.2	47.4	47.6	47.8	48.0
E	25.8	27.7	29.6	31.5	33.4	35.3

Which school(s) show a continual trend of improvement over the six years?

Question 5

The percentages of pupils achieving level 4 or above in English at the end of Key Stage 2 over a six-year period at an Academy chain are shown in the table.

School	2012	2013	2014	2015	2016	2017
A	41.6	41.9	42.4	42.5	43.1	43.6
B	37.1	37.3	37.3	37.5	37.9	38.4
C	40.6	41.2	41.8	42.4	43.0	43.6
D	47.0	46.2	47.4	47.6	47.8	48.0
E	25.8	27.7	29.6	31.5	33.4	35.3

Which school(s) show a consistent trend of improvement over the six years?

Question 6

A SENCO monitors the spelling age of eight pupils at two-monthly intervals over a year.

He records the spelling age minus actual age for each pupil.

Pupil	Spelling Age Minus Actual Age (Months)					
	September	November	January	March	May	July
A	-7	-5	-3	-1	1	3
B	2	3	3	2	4	5
C	-10	-8	-7	-4	-1	1
D	-3	-2	-1	1	1	1
E	0	-1	1	0	2	2
F	5	4	4	3	2	3
G	1	2	3	4	5	6
H	-8	-7	-5	-4	-2	-1

Which pupil made the greatest overall improvement between September and July?

Question 7

A SENCO monitors the spelling age of eight pupils at two-monthly intervals over a year.

He records the spelling age minus actual age for each pupil.

Pupil	Spelling Age Minus Actual Age (Months)					
	September	November	January	March	May	July
A	-7	-5	-3	-1	1	3
B	2	3	3	2	4	5
C	-10	-8	-7	-4	-1	1
D	-3	-2	-1	1	1	1
E	0	-1	1	0	2	2
F	5	4	4	3	2	3
G	1	2	3	4	5	6
H	-8	-7	-5	-4	-2	-1

What percentage of pupils had a trend of consistent improvement over this time?

Question 8

A head of a sixth form produced the following table to show performance in English A-Level from 2015 to 2017.

The table shows the percentage of candidates achieving each grade.

The percentages are rounded to the nearest whole number.

Year	Percentage of Candidates Achieving Each Grade							Total Number of Pupils
	A*	A	B	C	D	E	U	
2015	3	9	25	26	18	10	9	160
2016	5	11	28	35	13	7	1	200
2017	6	10	24	31	17	8	4	230

Indicate all true statements:

- The number of students who gained a grade A* increased each year.

- The number of students who gained a grade B increased each year.

- The number of students who gained a grade E increased by 50% from 2015 to 2017.

Question 9

Pupils in a primary school take a non-verbal reasoning test. Based on their school year and percentage test score, pupils are then given a standardised non-verbal reasoning rating that is calculated using the table below.

School Year	0-25%	26-40%	40-50%	50-60%	60-70%	70-85%	85-100%
Year 3	4	5	6	7	8	9	10
Year 4	3	4	5	6	7	8	9
Year 5	2	3	4	5	6	7	8
Year 6	1	2	3	4	5	6	7

What is the standardised rating of a year 4 pupil who scored 32 out of 40 on the non-verbal reasoning test?

Question 10

Pupils in a primary school take a non-verbal reasoning test. Based on their school year and percentage test score, pupils are then given a standardised non-verbal reasoning rating that is calculated using the table below.

School Year	0-25%	26-40%	41-50%	51-60%	61-70%	71-85%	86-100%
Year 3	4	5	6	7	8	9	10
Year 4	3	4	5	6	7	8	9
Year 5	2	3	4	5	6	7	8
Year 6	1	2	3	4	5	6	7

The table below shows the test scores and ages of six pupils.

Pupil	School Year	Test Score (out of 40)
A	Year 4	32
B	Year 5	30
C	Year 3	22
D	Year 5	18
E	Year 6	28
F	Year 3	12

What is the mean standardised non-verbal reasoning rating for this group of pupils?

Solutions

Fully worked solutions to all of these questions can be accessed at www.qtsskillstests.com/tables

On-Screen Questions

1) 7%

2) False, True, True

3) Child G

4) Schools A, C & E

5) Schools C & E

6) Pupil C

7) 25%

8) True, True, False

9) 8

10) 6

Bar Charts

Reading a Bar Chart

As well as reading tables, there are various types of graph that you need to be able to interpret data from. The first of these graphs is a bar chart.

The idea of a bar chart is to present the data using bars of differing heights to show the value of each category. On the side of the bar chart will be an axis that shows you what value is represented by what height.

For example, this bar chart shows what a group of year 11 leavers did after they left school

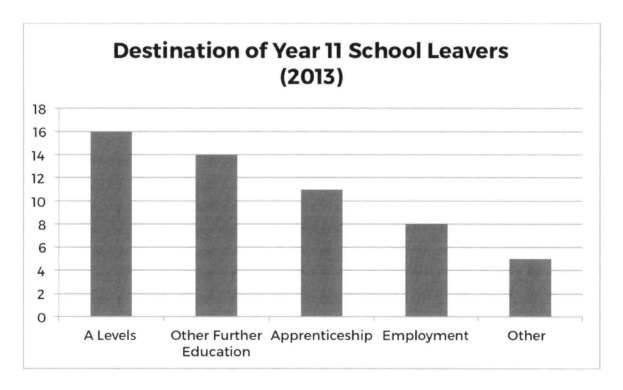

Notice that underneath each bar it tells you what the bar represents and by following the height of the bar along to the vertical axis you can see how many students chose that path. In the bar for 'other' the height falls in between the labels of '4' and '6' on the axis, showing this to be the next step for 5 students.

Multiple Data Sets

Sometimes a bar chart will be used to compare two (or more) different sets of data.

For example, the data in the bar chart above represents school leavers in 2013 and a school may wish to compare this data with the set of leavers in 2014. This will often be done using a multiple bar chart, in which the two sets of data are displayed side by side.

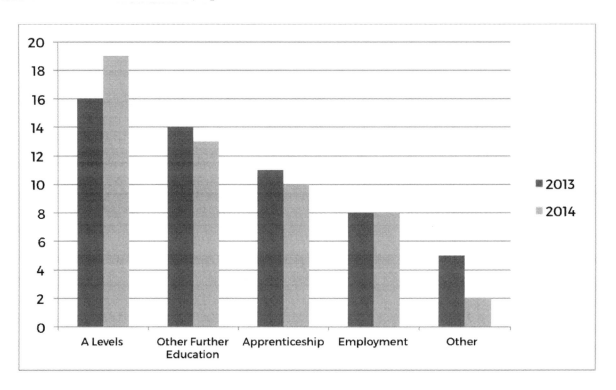

In this case, we can see that in 2013 there were 16 people who chose to do A Levels, but in 2014 this had increased to 19 people. For each option the left hand bar shows you how many chose that option in 2013 whereas the right hand bar shows how many chose it in 2014.

Top Tip

When a bar chart displays more than one type of data, it is important that you are clear what each bar shows. You will usually be given a key to help with this. In the example above, the key is to the right of the graph. Each of the years is displayed by a different shade, and the key shows which shade represents which year (this could also be shown by different colours or patterns). To find the data on the graph that represents a particular year, look for the bars that are in the appropriate shade.

Worked Example

A secondary school produces a bar chart to show the next step of school leavers in 2013 and 2014.

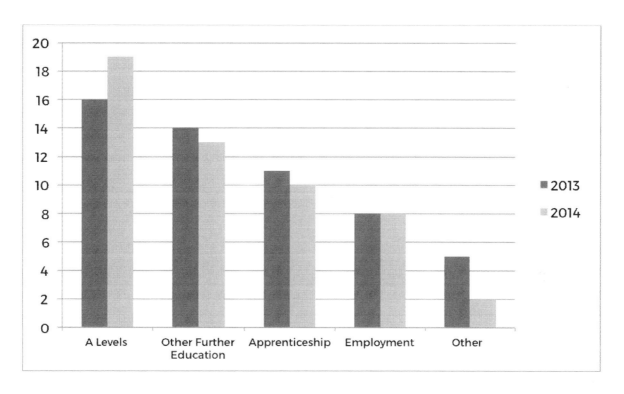

How many more people went into an apprenticeship than into employment in 2014?

As the question is asking about 2014, you will need to use the lighter grey bars. Read off the values from these bars for apprenticeships and employment.

The apprenticeship bar is level with the 10 on the vertical axis, and the employment bar is level with the 8.

This means that the number of people doing an apprenticeship more than going into employment will be 10 – 8 = 2.

Answer: 2

Stacked Bar Charts

Whilst a multiple bar chart can be great for comparing two sets of data, sometimes it is more useful to see the combined effect of the data. In this case, you would use a composite bar chart, where the bars for 2014 are stacked on top of those for 2013.

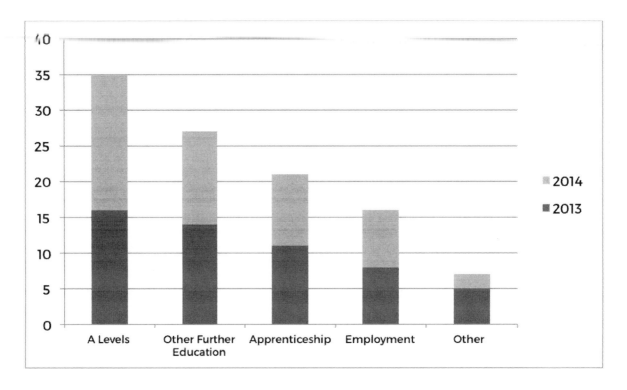

This time you can easily compare the numbers of people taking each route over the combined two-year period. For example, there were 35 people who went on to do A Levels in total.

It is also possible on a composite bar chart to break down the individual values. The key tells you which shade represents each year. Looking at just the part of the 'other further education' bar that is shaded for 2013 we can see that this part of the bar stops at 14, so 14 people took this route in 2013.

Finding the 2014 value is slightly more complex. You need to take note of both where the bar starts and where it finishes. For example, the 2014 apprenticeship bar starts at 11 and extends up to 21. To work out the number of people going on to do an apprenticeship in 2014, you need to find the difference between these two numbers. 21 − 11 = 10, so 10 students chose this option.

Worked Example

A school compiled a bar chart to show the end of key stage 2 levels in English for a group of children.

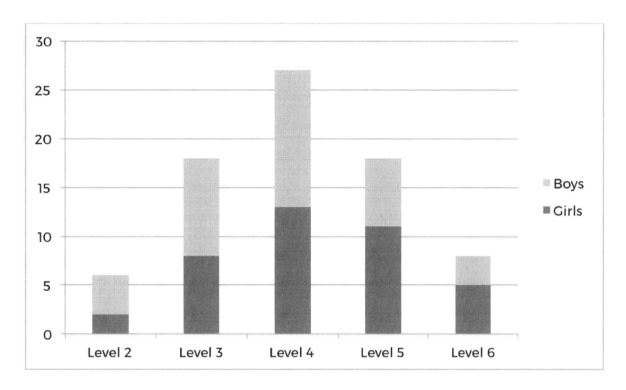

What was the proportion of boys in the group?

The first step is to work out the total number of students in the group. To do this, look at the total height of each bar and add the answers together. This gives 6 + 18 + 27 + 18 + 8 = 77.

Next, work out the total number of boys. The key shows that boys are represented by the light grey sections, which are the top section of each bar, so you will need to find the difference between where that section starts and where it finishes:

For Level 2 the light grey section starts at 2 and finishes at 6, so the number of boys is 6 – 2 = 4.

For Level 3 it starts at 8 and finishes at 18, so the number of boys is 18 – 8 = 10.

For Level 4 it starts at 13 and finishes at 27, so the number of boys is 27 – 13 = 14.

For Level 5 it starts at 11 and finishes at 18, so the number of boys is 18 – 11 = 7.

For Level 6 it starts at 5 and finishes at 8 so the number of boys is 8 – 5 = 3.

The total number of boys can be found by adding these values together.

4 + 10 + 14 + 7 + 3 = 38

The proportion of boys is 38 out of 77, which can be written as the fraction $^{38}/_{77}$.

Answer: $^{38}/_{77}$

Horizontal Bar Charts

It is possible that you may be given a bar chart with horizontal bars instead of vertical. In this case the numbered axis would be on the bottom and the bars would go from left to right.

For example, if the bar chart shown at the start of this chapter about school leavers was displayed as a horizontal bar chart, this is how it would look.

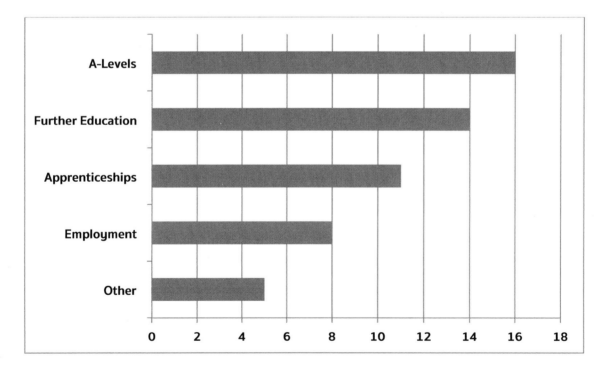

Again, you may see this kind of chart with multiple data sets presented next to each other, or they may be stacked (this time they would be stacked horizontally). To extract data from this kind of horizontal bar chart, you can use exactly the same methods we have discussed in this chapter. It doesn't make any difference whether the bars are vertical or horizontal.

Sometimes you may see a horizontal bar chart (or even a vertical one) where the data is not presented as an absolute amount but rather as a percentage of a total.

For example, the bar chart below shows the end of KS2 English levels of three classes of children.

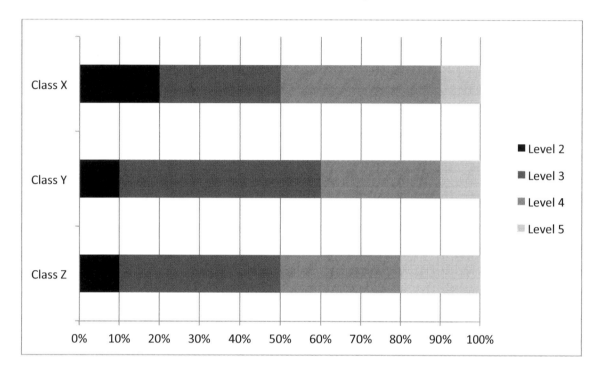

You can see from this that 20% of children in Class X were level 2, as were 10% of children in each of Class Y and Class Z (to work out exactly how many children this is, you would need to know the total number of children in each class).

To work out the percentage of children that got the other levels, work out the difference between the two ends of that section of the bar. For example, in Class X the section of the bar for 'Level 3' begins at 20% and ends at 50%, so this would represent 50% - 20% = 30% of the class.

Worked Example

A primary school produces a bar chart to show the end of KS2 English levels of three classes. There were 30 children in each class.

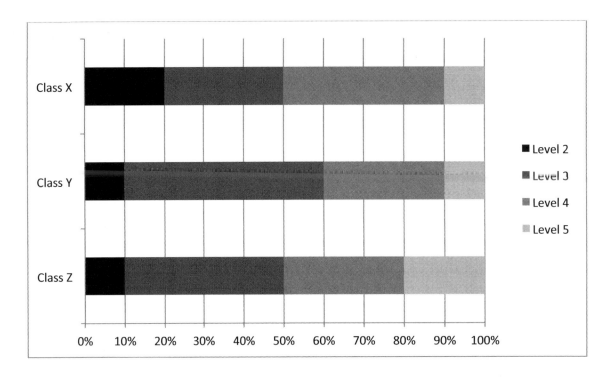

Altogether, how many children got level 4?

Work out the number of children from each class in turn.

For Class X, the Level 4 bar begins at 50% and ends at 90%, so this represents 90% - 50% = 40% of the class. 40% of 30 is 12 children.

For Class Y, the Level 4 bar begins at 60% and ends at 90%, so this represents 90% - 60% = 30% of the class. 30% of 30 is 9 children.

For Class Z, the Level 4 bar begins at 50% and ends at 80%, so this represents 80% - 50% = 30% of the class. 30% of 30 is 9 children.

Altogether, this is a total of 12 + 9 + 9 = 30 children.

Answer: 30

Averages From Bar Charts

If you are asked to find an average or a range from a bar chart, your first step is to use the bar chart to find the original data and then use these values for your calculation.

For the range, you need to use the labels on the bars (not the heights of the bars) to work out the highest and lowest values and subtract them from each other.

For the mode, you are interested in the most frequent outcome, so look for which bar has the greatest height.

For the mean, the height tells you the frequency, so multiply this by the value the bar represents. Add these values up and then divide by the total frequency.

It is less likely that you will be asked to find the median from a bar chart. If you do need to do it, you could use the bar chart to find each value and write them in a table. Once you have done this, you can work out the median as described in the 'Averages & Range' chapter.

Worked Example

A primary school produces a bar chart to show the end of KS2 English levels of Class Y.

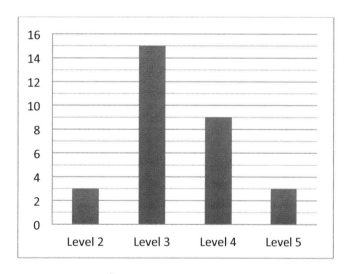

What is (a) the range; (b) the mode; (c) the mean; and (d) the median of the levels?

The range is the highest level minus the lowest level. The highest level is the right hand bar (5) and the lowest level is the left hand bar (2) so the range is 5 – 2 = 3.

The mode is the most frequently attained level, which will be represented by the highest bar. In this case, the mode is level 3.

To find the mean, multiply each level by its frequency and divide by the total frequency (which is 3 + 15 + 9 + 3 = 30).

(2 × 3) + (3 × 15) + (4 × 9) + (5 × 3) = 102 ÷ 30 = 3.4

For the median, if the total frequency is 30, the halfway people will be the 15th and 16th. As there are 3 people in level 2, and the next 15 people are in level 3 (making 18 altogether), the 15th and 16th people will be amongst those who got level 3.

Answer: (a) 3; (b) 3; (c) 3.4; (d) 3

Practice Questions on Bar Charts

Question 1

This bar chart shows the number of children who achieved a special performance award at five different schools.

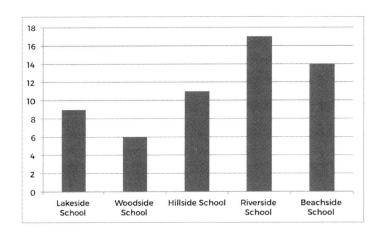

What was the mean number of children that won the award from each school?

Question 2

A bar chart was constructed to show the optional GCSE subjects chosen by students in 2012, 2013 and 2014.

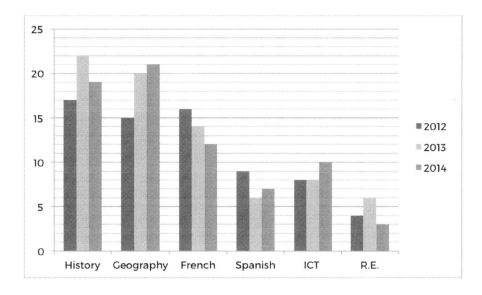

Indicate all true statements:

- History was the most popular subject every year.
- There were no subjects for which the numbers declined every year.
- ICT was more popular than R.E. every year.

Question 3

A primary school surveyed the lunchtime habits of its children and made a bar chart to show the percentage of boys and girls that had school lunch, brought a packed lunch, and went home for lunch.

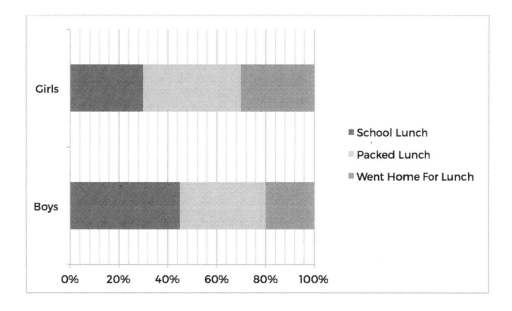

Altogether there were 70 girls and 80 boys in the school.

What percentage of students went home for lunch?

Give your answer to one decimal place.

Question 4

The number of subjects being studied by the students in a sixth form is represented by this bar chart:

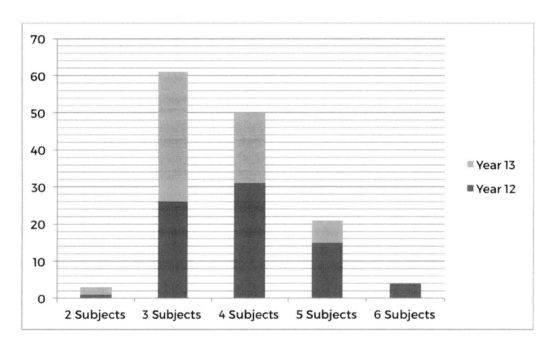

Indicate all true statements:

- The mean number of subjects per student in total is 3.7 (to 1 decimal place)
- There are more students of each year doing 3 subjects than any other number of subjects.
- There are a total of 77 students in year 13.

Question 5

The grades of a group of students on the two papers of a French exam are shown on the bar chart below.

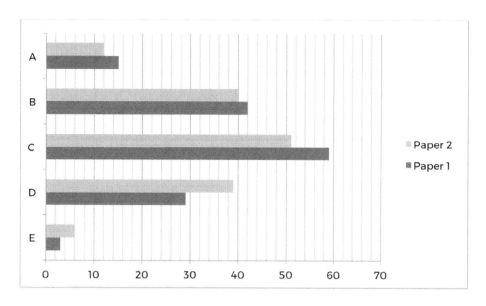

What was the difference between the percentages of students who got a C on the two papers?

Give your answer to the nearest whole number.

Question 6

A group of year 9 students were asked to choose which subject to study at GCSE level. Their choices are shown in a bar chart.

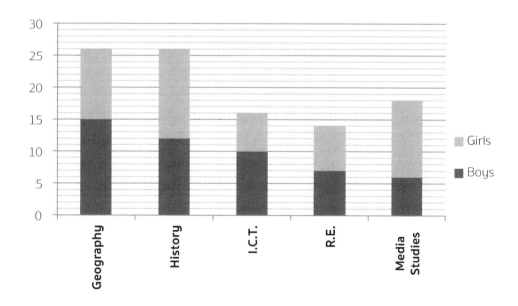

Indicate all true statements:

- The most popular subject for girls was also the most popular subject for boys.

- 24% of girls chose Media Studies.

- The same percentage of boys and girls chose R.E.

Question 7

A sixth-form college produces a bar chart to track the number of students taking A-Levels in core subjects over a three-year period.

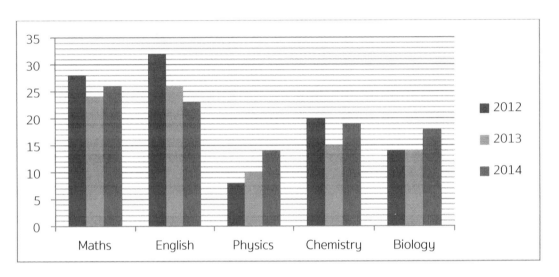

For which subject was the range of numbers of students highest?

Question 8

A science teacher produces a bar chart to show the levels achieved by students in their class at the end of Key Stage 3.

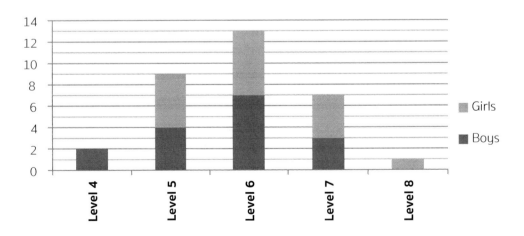

What percentage of girls achieved level 6 or above?

Question 9

This graph shows the levels achieved in Maths at the end of Key Stage 3 by 76 students in 2016 and 87 students in 2017.

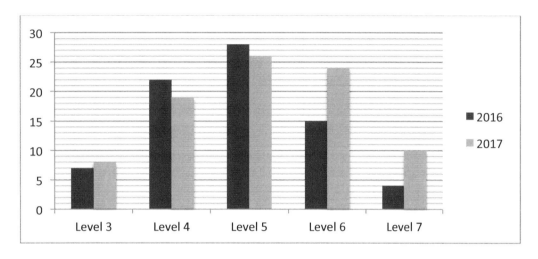

What was the difference in the percentage of students achieving level 5 or above in 2017 compared to 2016?

Give your answer to 1 decimal place.

Question 10

A primary school tracks the secondary schools that year 6 leavers move on to over a three-year period.

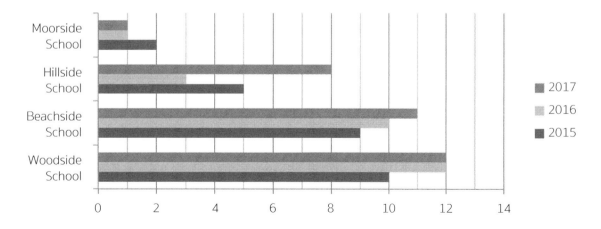

Indicate all true statements:

- Every year, Woodside School was the modal choice.

- The range of the number of students choosing Hillside School was 3.

- The mean number of students choosing Beachside School was 10.

Solutions

Fully worked solutions to all of these questions can be accessed at <u>www.qtsskillstests.com/barcharts</u>

On-Screen Questions

1) 11.4

2) False, False, True

3) 24.7%

4) True, False, False

5) 5%

6) False, True, True

7) English

8) 68.75%

9) 7.2%

10) True, False, True

Line Graphs

Using Line Graphs

Another type of graph that you will need to be familiar with is the line graph. These are visual representations of how one variable causes another variable to change.

Usually (though not always) the horizontal axis will represent time and the vertical axis will represent something that you want to measure.

In the example below, the vertical axis represents the percentage of children achieving Level 5 in English at the end of KS2 and the horizontal axis represents the different years.

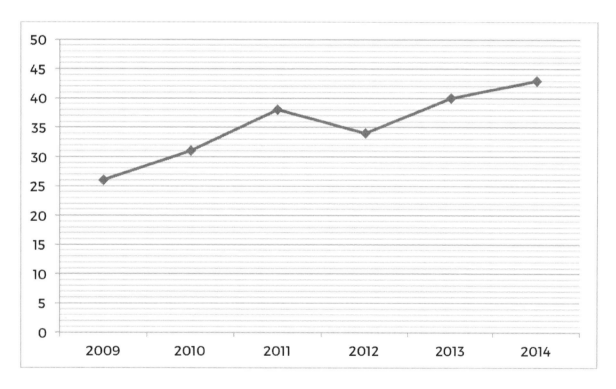

The line shows the trend in the results. Where the line goes up it shows the results are improving, and where the line goes down the results are getting worse.

To find the percentage for a given year, look at the part of the line that is directly above that year, and follow it along in a straight line to the vertical axis to see the number of students represented.

For example, in 2010 the percentage is represented by the second of the markers on the line. Looking along to the vertical axis, this would suggest that 31% of students achieved level 5 that year.

Not all line graphs have the markers on the line to help you read the relevant points. If you are given a line graph without the markers, finding where the line changes direction in that year can show you where to look. If the line does not change direction in that section, then use the point directly above the middle of the section.

Multiple Line Graphs

It is also possible that you will be given a line graph with more than one line for you to compare. If this happens, you can treat each line separately and read off the data as though it is the only line on the graph.

Worked Example

A primary school produced a line graph to show the percentages of children achieving level 5 in English and Maths at the end of Key Stage 2.

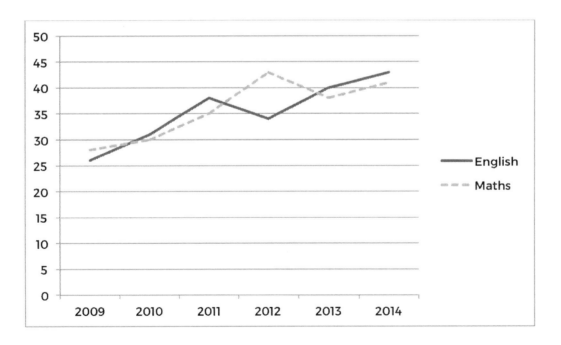

In which year was the percentage of children that got level 5 in Maths lower than it was the year before?

The key on the right hand side of the graph tells you that the solid line shows results in English and the dashed line shows results in Maths. We need to focus on the dashed line.

To see which year got a lower percentage than the year before, we look for where the dashed line started to go down.

This happened between 2012 and 2013, so the year where the percentage was worse than the year before is 2013.

Answer: 2013

Top Tip

Sometimes you may have a line graph where the axis does not start at zero. When this happens, do not worry about the values that have been 'skipped' – you can use whatever values you read off on the axes.

Line Graphs With Points

Sometimes you may be given a line graph that also has some points marked on the graph that are not on the line. In this case, the line will display a general trend (perhaps an average) whilst the points by themselves would show values for specific individual cases. Any individual points that are higher on the graph than the line show individuals that performed above average. Points below the line represent below average performance.

Worked Example

A school produced a line graph to show the average percentage score of each year group on a Maths test. The graph also shows the score of a Gifted and Talented pupil named Sonia.

By how much was Sonia's score higher than the average for her year group?

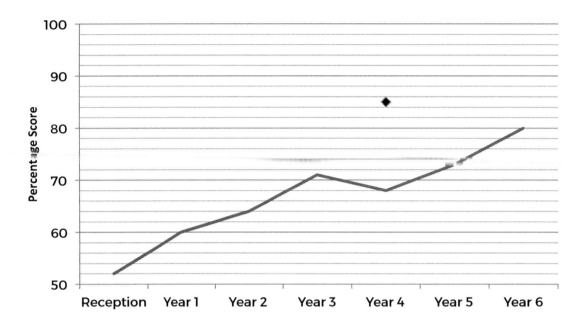

Sonia's score is represented by the individual point shown on the graph. From this point you can read down to 'year 4' on the horizontal axis to show which year Sonia is in, and read across to '85' on the vertical axis to see her score.

You need to compare this to the average score for year 4. To do this, read across to the vertical axis from the point on the line that is directly above where it says 'year 4'. This shows an average score of 68.

Sonia's score was above the average by 85 – 68 = 17 marks.

Answer: 17

Practice Questions on Line Graphs

Question 1

A Maths department compiled a line graph to show the percentage of students that achieved a GCSE grade C or above in each of the 8 maths sets in the year group.

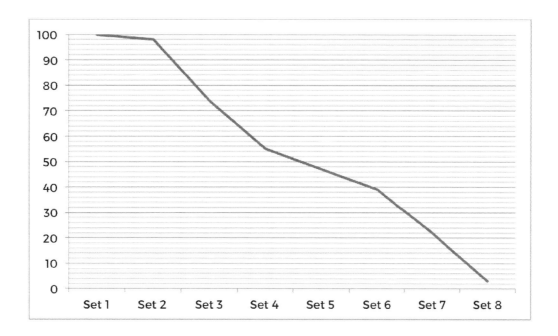

Which was the lowest set that had over half of the students achieve grade C or above?

Question 2

A sixth form college tracked the percentage of leavers going on to further education and to full time employment over a five year period.

They displayed their findings in the line graph below.

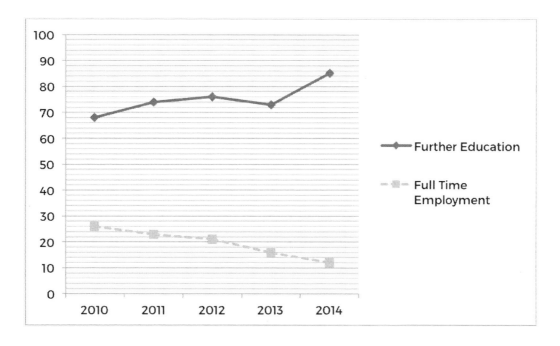

By how many percentage points had the difference between those going on to further education and those going on to full time employment increased over the 5-year period?

Question 3

A school tracked the average score of 5 year groups in a spelling test, and compared these scores with a random sample of 4 students.

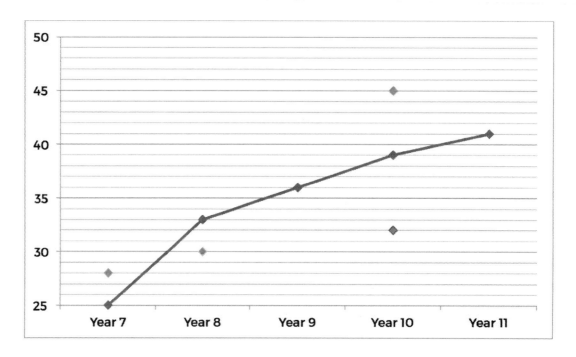

Indicate all true statements.

- Each year group had a higher average score than the year below.
- The average score for year 7 was zero.
- The sample student with the lowest score was above average for their year.

Question 4

The percentage of students achieving 5 or more GCSEs at A*-C grades was compared for 3 local schools over a 5 year period.

The results are displayed in a line graph.

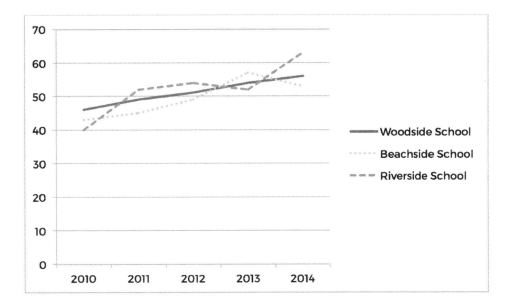

Indicate all true statements.

- Beachside School was the only school in which the results improved every year.
- Each of the schools had at least one year in which it out-performed the other two schools.
- There was no year in which Riverside School was the second best performing school.

Question 5

For five consecutive years, a primary school held a fundraiser and recorded the average amount of money raised per child on the line graph below.

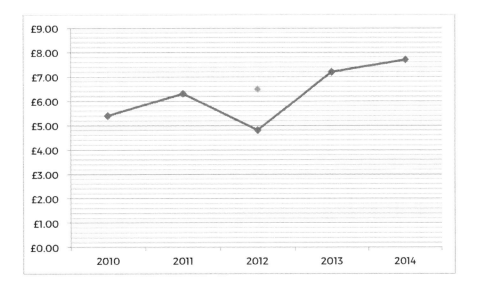

One particular child is also highlighted on the graph.

Assuming the same number of children took part in the fundraiser each year, how much more than the overall mean did this child raise?

Question 6

A class of students was asked to take a mental arithmetic test each year throughout their time at a primary school. The average score for the class was plotted in a line graph.

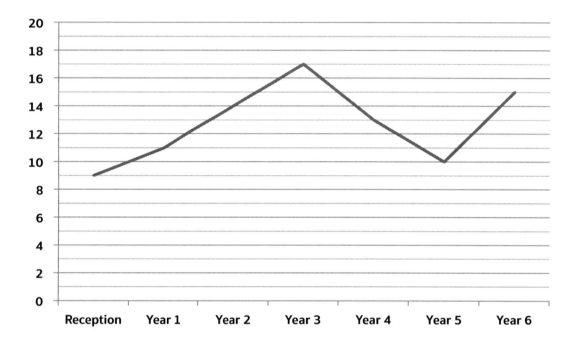

In year 5, Johnny was three marks below the class average and in year 6, he was three marks above the class average.

How many marks did Johnny improve by from year 5 to year 6?

Question 7

A school produced a line graph to track the percentage of students achieving level 5 in Maths, English and Science at the end of KS2 over a 5 year period.

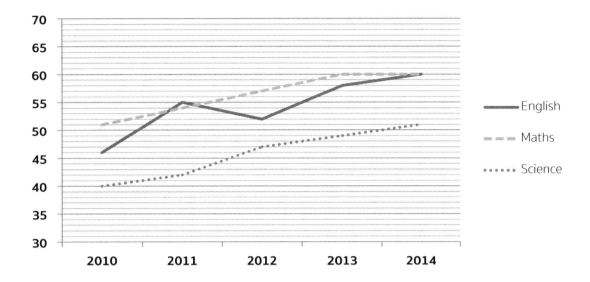

Indicate all true statements:

- Science is the only subject for which the percentage increased each year.

- English is the only subject for which the percentage decreased each year.

- Every year there was a higher percentage of students achieving level 5 in Maths than in any other subject.

Question 8

A school monitors the total number of days of unauthorised absence in a 12-week term from each year group.

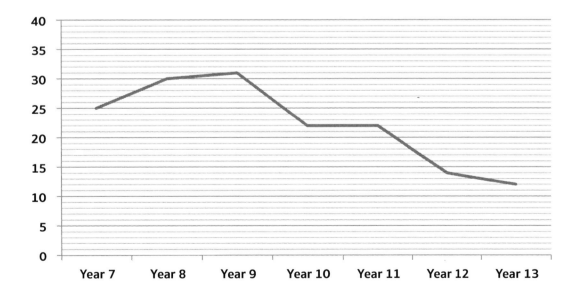

What was the mean number of unauthorised absences each week across the school?

Question 9

A student took a spelling test each week over a term and her scores were plotted on a line graph.

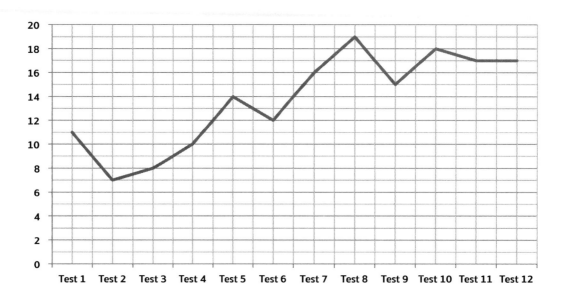

What was the range of her scores?

Question 10

Five students take an English test every half-term. Their scores are shown on a line graph.

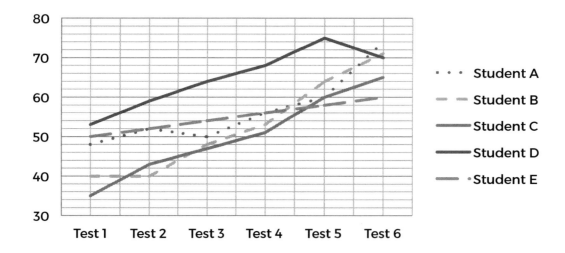

Which student(s) had a trend of continual improvement in their scores?

Solutions

Fully worked solutions to all of these questions can be accessed at www.qtsskillstests.com/linegraphs

On-Screen Questions

1) Set 4

2) 31

3) True, False, True

4) False, True, True

5) 22p

6) 11

7) True, False, False

8) 13

9) 12

10) Students C & E

Pie Charts

Interpreting Pie Charts

Pie charts visually display the proportions of a total that are in different categories. They do this by dividing up a full circle (or 'pie') into appropriately sized portions.

For example, if a quarter of students got a grade C on a test, this would be represented by a quarter of the circle. If a third of the students got a B then this would be represented by a third of the circle.

This can be seen in the following example.

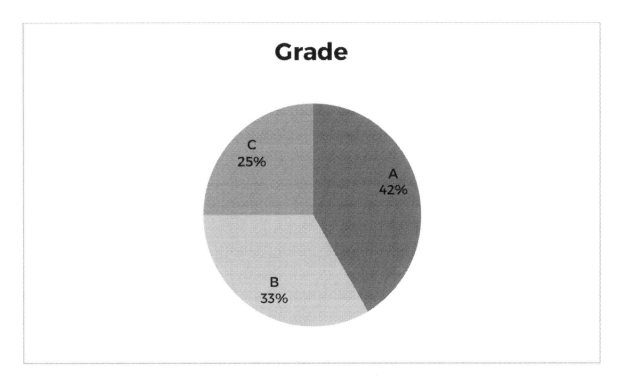

To understand a pie chart, you need to know what proportion of the pie chart is in each category.

There are four ways you may be expected to do this:

- Some proportions can be observed visually. For example, if half or a quarter of the circle is in a specific category, this is usually evident from the pie chart.

- Sometimes the proportions will be indicated in the sections of the pie chart. These would usually be given as percentages of the full amount, but could also be given as decimals or fractions.

- Sometimes you may be told the number of people/things that each section represents. In this case you can work out the proportion by dividing this number by the total of all the sections of the pie chart.

- You may be given the number of degrees in each section. In this case you can work out the proportion by making a fraction with the full 360° of the circle as the denominator, so a 40° section would represent $^{40}/_{360}$ of the total amount, which can be simplified to $^{1}/_{9}$

If you are asked to use the pie chart to find the amount of people or things in a category, then you will need to know the total amount that the pie chart represents. In the example above where a section of the pie was 40°, if you knew that the total amount represented by the pie chart was 45, then you could work out the number represented by the given section by finding $^{1}/_{9}$ of 45, giving an answer of 5.

Worked Example

A primary school produces a pie chart to show what secondary school year 6 leavers go on to.

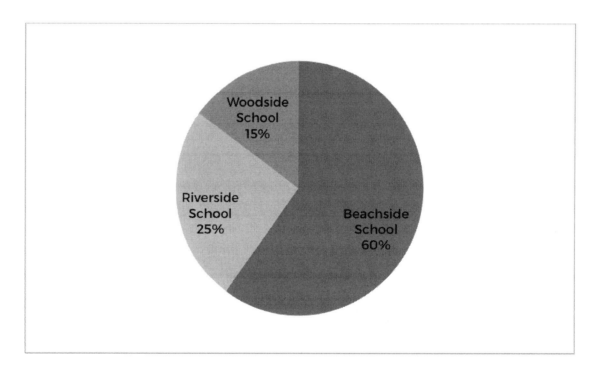

If 60 students left the primary school altogether, how many of those students went to Woodside School?

The section of the pie chart for 'Woodside School' is 15% of the total.

Given that there are 60 students altogether, you will need to find 15% of 60. This would give 60 ÷ 100 × 15 = 9 students.

Answer: 9

Working Out Full Amounts From One Section

Sometimes you may not be given the total represented by the pie chart, but instead be given the value represented by one section. In this case you can divide the amount specified for the section by the percentage of the whole that section is worth (which would give you 1% of the total) and then multiply this by 100 to get the full amount.

Worked Example

A drama group in a junior school produces a pie chart to show the year groups that their members belong to.

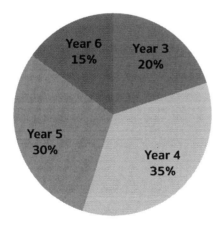

If there were 8 children from year 3, how many children were in the drama club altogether?

Start by dividing the number of children specified for year 3 (8) by the percentage represented by that section (20%).

8 ÷ 20 = 0.4

This is 1% of the total, so to find the total you can multiply it by 100.

0.4 × 100 = 40

Answer: 40

Top Tip

Be careful when you are asked to compare two (or more) pie charts. Just because a segment on one of the pie charts is bigger than a segment on the other one, it does not necessarily represent more people/things. This is because pie charts show proportion, not overall amounts. If you have two pie charts where the first represents a total of 180 people and the second represents 60 people, then a quarter of the first one (45 people) will be worth more than half of the second one (30 people), even though the segment will look smaller.

Practice Questions on Pie Charts

Question 1

This pie chart shows the grades achieved by 75 students in one school in A-Level Spanish.

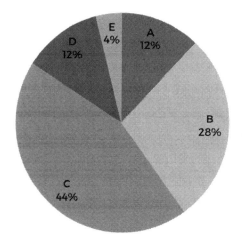

How many students got grade C or above?

Question 2

A college created a pie chart to show which Science subjects were chosen as A-Level subjects in a given year group.

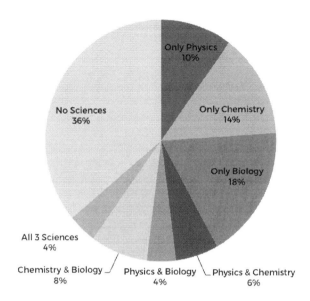

Altogether there were 250 students in the college.

How many of them took Physics?

Question 3

A group of year 5 students were asked to name their favourite author.

The results are shown in this pie chart.

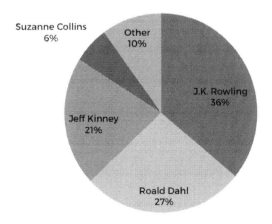

162 children chose Roald Dahl.

How many chose Jeff Kinney?

Question 4

A school wanted to track the next step of those leaving the school with 5 or more A*-C GCSEs (60 students) and of those without (80 students).

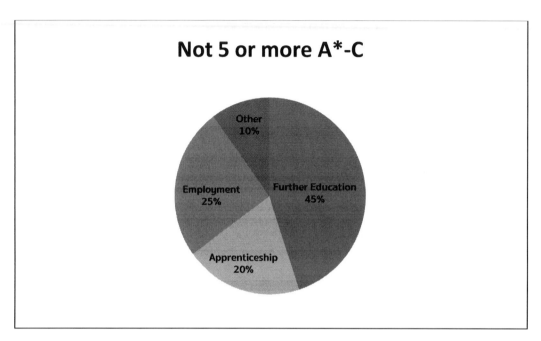

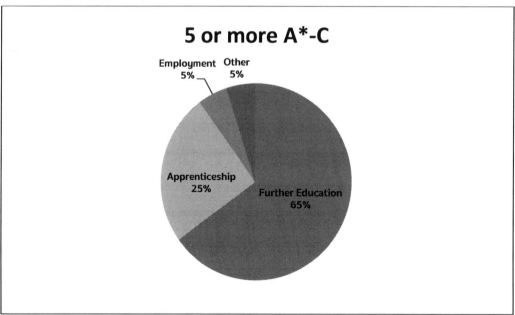

Indicate all true statements:

- The mode is the same for both groups.

- The number of people who got 5 or more A*-Cs going on to apprenticeships is the same as the number without 5 or more A*-Cs going on to employment.

- Over half of the people doing apprenticeships got 5 or more A*-Cs.

Question 5

In year 10 at Woodside School are 180 students and at Beachside School are 160 students. Both schools produced pie charts showing the proportion of students studying languages.

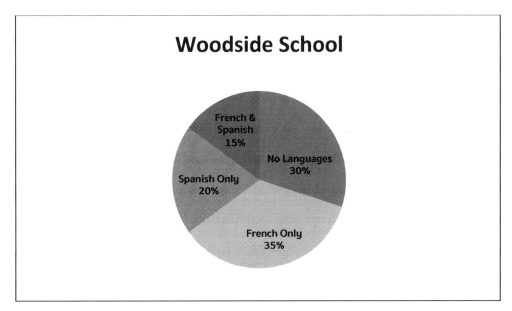

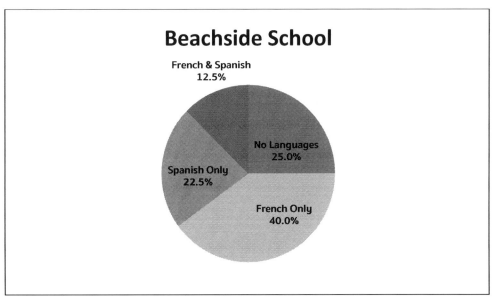

How many more people are studying both languages at Woodside School than at Beachside School?

Question 6

A junior school chooses 60 children to represent it at a regional mathematics competition.

The year groups of the students are shown in the pie chart below.

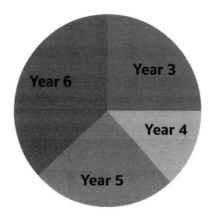

What was the modal number of students in a year group representing the school?

Question 7

A school inspection observed 36 lessons in a primary school.

Four lessons were considered to be unsatisfactory.

How many lessons were considered to be good or outstanding?

Question 8

Woodside Primary School produces a bar chart to show which secondary schools their year 6 leavers go on to.

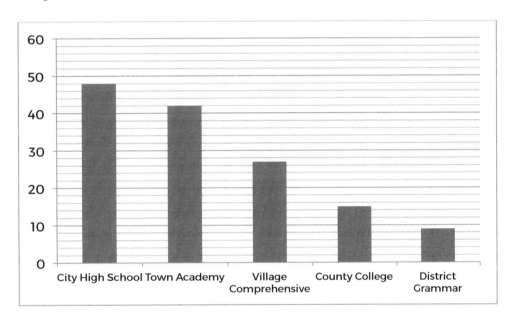

Town Academy produces a pie chart to show which schools their new intake arrived from.

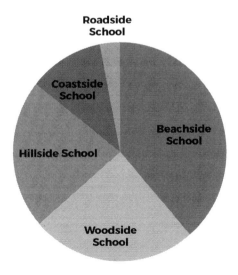

What is the total number of students in this intake?

Question 9

A sixth-form college produced a pie chart to show the number of A-Levels studied by different students at the college.

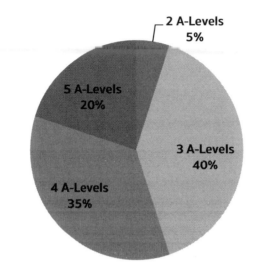

There are 120 students in the college. How many A-Levels are being studied in total?

Question 10

A school produced pie charts to show the percentages of students in years 10 and 11 that are studying for the higher tier exam in English Language and in English Literature.

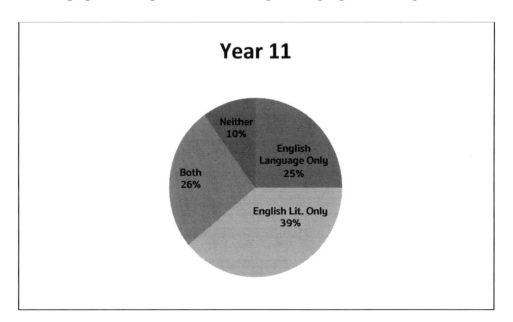

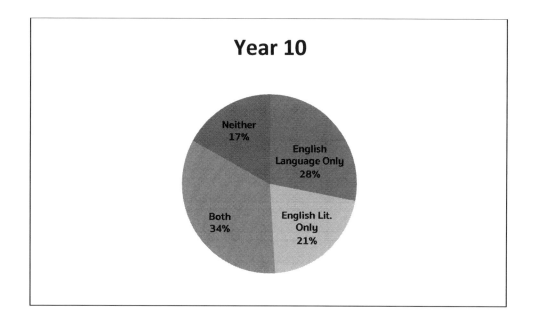

What is the percentage point increase in the number of students doing higher tier in English Language from year 11 to year 10?

Solutions

Fully worked solutions to all of these questions can be accessed at www.qtsskillstests.com/piecharts

On-Screen Questions

1) 63

2) 60

3) 126

4) True, False, False

5) 7

6) 15

7) 14

8) 168

9) 444

10) 11%

Scatter Graphs

Reading Scatter Graphs

Scatter graphs compare two categories by showing a series of points (these could be dots or crosses) in different places on a grid. The horizontal axis represents one category and the vertical axis represents the other category. Each of the points represents an individual case, and the values for that case can be found by reading along and down to the two axes.

For example, the scatter graph below compares the percentages students scored in a mock exam with the percentages they scored in the final exam.

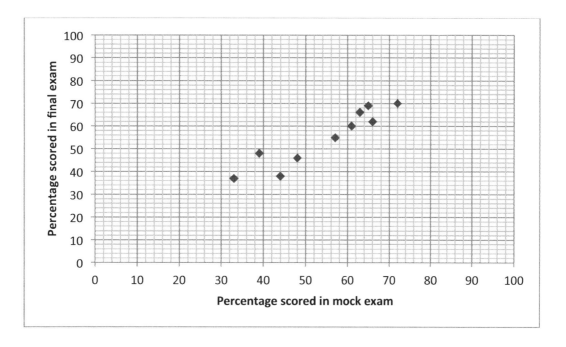

Each dot represents the scores of a different student. For example, the dot closest to the bottom left corner of the graph represents a student who scored 33 on the mock exam and 37 on the final exam.

Worked Example

A teacher produces a scatter graph to show the percentage scores of a group of students in a mock exam and in a final exam (scatter graph shown above).

One student scored 61 marks in the mock exam. What was their score in the final exam?

The horizontal axis represents the mock exam, so find 61 on this axis and then look for a point on the graph that is directly above this value. There is one such point (marked with an outline on the diagram).

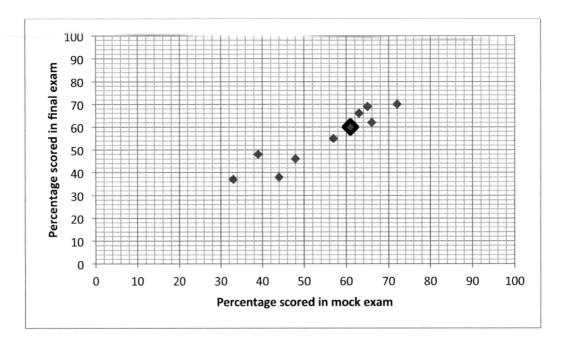

From this point, read along to the vertical axis to see the score of this student on the final exam. This score would be 60.

Answer: 60

Comparing Values Using Scatter Graphs

When you are asked to compare two categories on a scatter graph that use the same scale, rather than checking each point individually, you could draw a straight line that goes through all the points where both axes show the same value (this line may sometimes be already drawn for you). You can then use this line to make the comparison.

If you are asked how many did better in one category than the other, then see how many points are above the line (these are better at the category on the vertical axis) or below the line (these are better at the category on the horizontal axis).

Anyone exactly on the line scored the same in both categories.

If you are asked who changed by most, then see which point is furthest from the line (or if it is asking who improved the most, do the same ensuring the point is on the correct side of the line to show an improvement).

Top Tip

The line that is drawn for this kind of problem is not the same as a line of best fit. A line of best fit would always go through the middle of the data. The line that we are using here is a line that indicates where both scores would be the same. It is possible that all the scores could end up on the same side of this line.

Worked Example

A school produced a scatter graph to compare the percentages a group of students scored in a mock exam with the percentages they scored in a final exam. How many students scored higher in the final exam than in the mock?

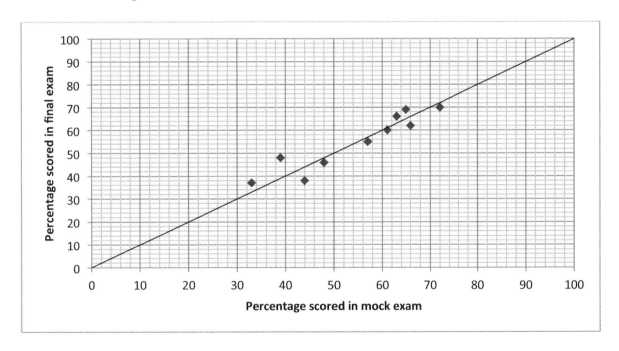

The line is drawn through the points where students scored the same on both exams.

Any points above the line score better on the final exam, so to find out how many did best on this exam, count how many such points there are.

You can see on the graph that there are four points above the line, so the answer is four students.

Answer: 4

Correlation

A scatter graph can be used to work out whether there is a link between the two categories (i.e. whether a high score in one of the categories would make a high score in the other category more or less likely).

There are three possible links:

• They could be linked so that as one value increases, the other is likely to increase as well. This is called positive correlation and can be seen by a set of points that roughly form a diagonal pattern from the bottom left of the graph to the top right, as in the example above.

• They could be linked so that as one value increases the other decreases (for example, as the number of days missed through absence increases, the scores achieved on a test are likely to decrease). This is called negative correlation and can be seen by a set of points that roughly form a diagonal pattern from the top left of the graph to the bottom right.

• They may not be linked at all. This is called no correlation and can be seen when there is no pattern in the points on the graph.

Worked Example

A teacher produces a scatter graph to show the percentage scores of a group of students in a mock exam and in a final exam.

What (if any) correlation does the scatter graph show?

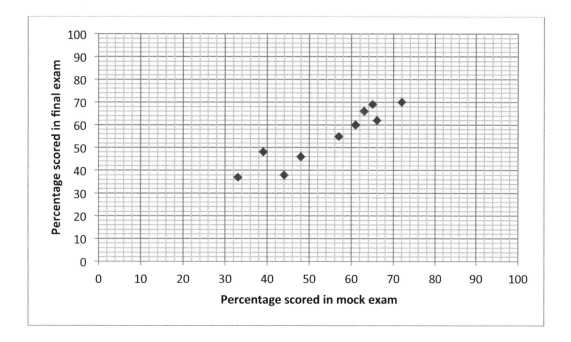

The points on the scatter graph form a rough diagonal from the bottom left of the graph to the top right. This is a positive correlation.

Answer: Positive Correlation

Averages From Scatter Graphs

You may be asked to work out a statistical measure from a scatter graph.

- If you need to work out the range, the graph can show you the highest and lowest points. Look up the values for these points and subtract them.

- If you need to find the median, you can find the middle point on the graph and look up its value (make sure you know which of the categories you are looking for the median in – the middle point measured on the vertical axis won't necessarily be the middle point on the horizontal axis).

- If you need to find the mode, look for which value has the most points at that value.

- If you are asked to find the mean, you will need to find the numerical value for each point, add up the values and divide by how many values there are.

Worked Example

A teacher produces a scatter graph to show the percentage scores of a group of students in a mock exam and in a final exam.

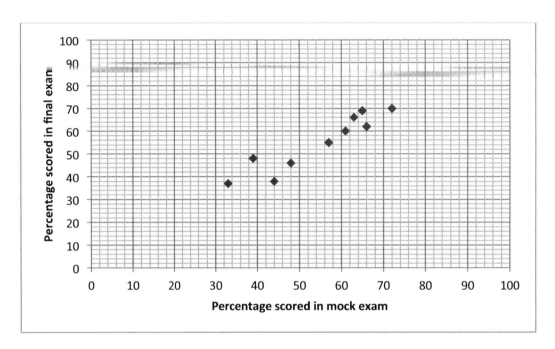

Find (a) the range for the mock exam, and (b) the median score for the final exam.

Because part (a) asks about the mock exam, you will need to use the values on the horizontal axis to work out the range (had it asked about the final exam, you would use the values on the vertical axis).

You need to find the difference between the values of the points to the very left and very right of the graph.

The left hand point has a value of 33 and the right hand point has a value of 72, so the range is 72 – 33 = 39

Part (b) asks about the final exam, so this time you will need to use the values from the vertical axis. Because you are working out the median value, you need to find the middle point when counting from bottom to top. Altogether, there are 10 points on the graph. The median will be halfway between the 5th and 6th points.

The 5th point from the bottom is 55, and the 6th point from the bottom is 60, so the median will be (55 + 60) ÷ 2 = 57.5

Answer: (a) 39 and (b) 57.5

Practice Questions on Scatter Graphs

Question 1

A local authority produces a scatter graph to compare the percentage of students achieving A*-C in their Maths GCSE with the percentage achieving A*-C in English in 9 schools in their region.

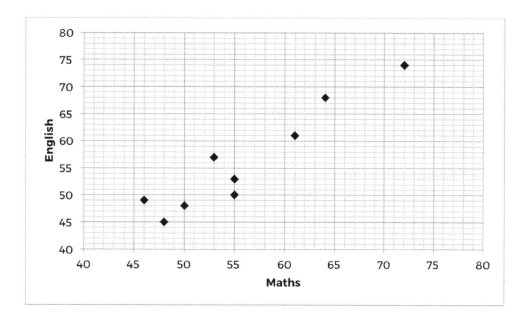

What was the mean score in English across the nine schools?

Give your answer to the nearest whole number.

Question 2

A local authority produces a scatter graph to compare the percentage of students achieving A*-C in their Maths GCSE with the percentage achieving A*-C in English in 9 schools in their region.

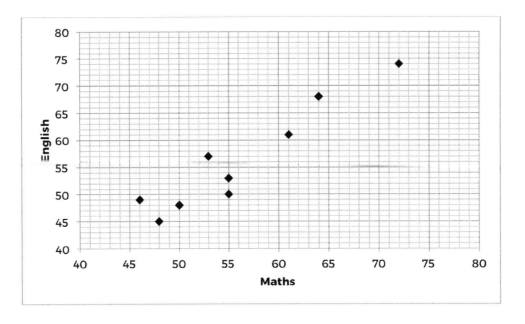

What percentage of schools performed better in English than in Maths?

Give your answer to the nearest whole number.

Question 3

A junior school produces a scatter graph to compare the scores students achieved in a year 6 spelling test with the scores they had achieved in another spelling test when they were in year 4.

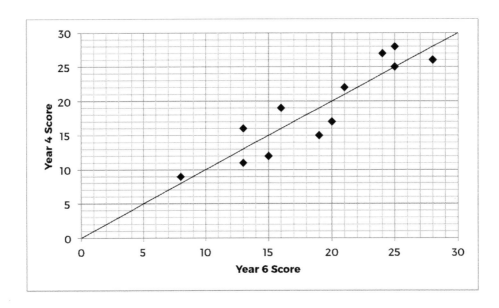

How many students scored higher on the year 6 test than on the year 4 test?

Question 4

A scatter graph is produced to compare students' percentage scores in a Spanish written exam and a Spanish listening exam.

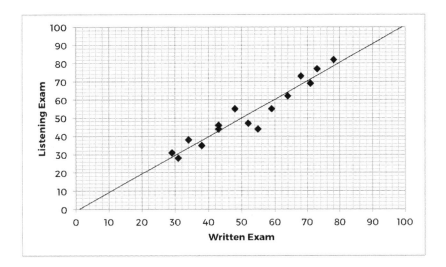

Indicate all true statements:

- The written exam had a higher range of scores than the listening exam.
- The median scores for both exams were the same.
- There was a student who achieved the mode score on both exams.

Question 5

A scatter graph is produced to compare the scores children scored in a Maths test with the number of push-ups they were able to complete in a P.E. lesson.

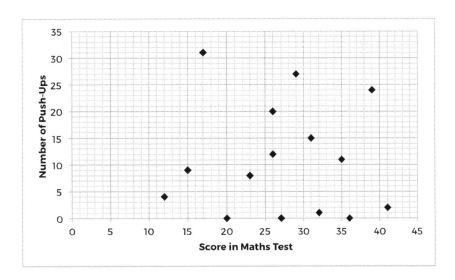

How many students scored above the median in both the maths test and the push-ups?

Question 6

A maths department tracked the score achieved by a group of year 10 students on a calculator and a non-calculator paper in a mock exam.

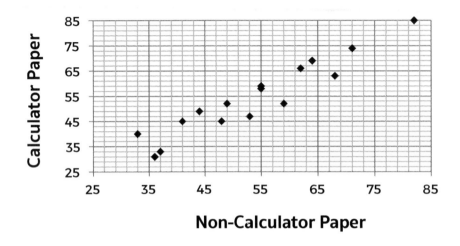

What percentage of students achieved a higher score on the calculator paper?

Question 7

The scores achieved in science by a group of year 8 students on a practical and on a written exam are displayed on a scatter diagram.

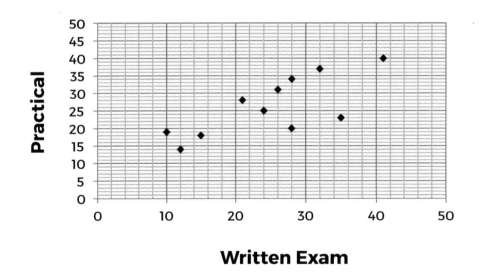

How many students scored above the median on both the practical and the written exam?

Question 8

Eight students took a spelling test (out of 20) and a maths test (out of 50). Their results are shown on a scatter graph.

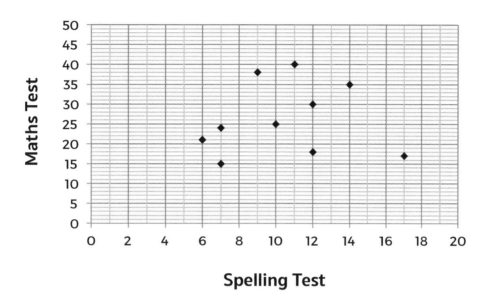

Spelling Test

How many students achieved the same percentage score on both tests?

Question 9

A French department gave children a speaking test and a vocabulary test (both were out of 20). They plotted the results on a scatter graph.

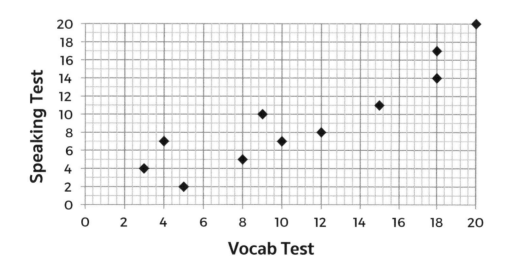

Vocab Test

What was the difference between the median scores for the two tests?

Question 10

A French department gave children a speaking test and a vocabulary test (both were out of 20). They plotted the results on a scatter graph.

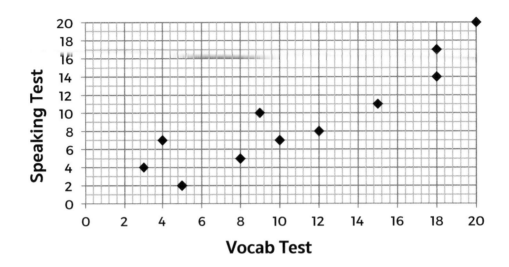

Indicate all true statements:

- No students got the same score on both tests.

- Over 60% of students did better on the vocab test than on the speaking test.

- The modal score for the vocab test was 8.

Solutions

Fully worked solutions to all of these questions can be accessed at www.qtsskillstests.com/scattergraphs

On-Screen Questions

1) 56

2) 44%

3) 5

4) False, False, True

5) 4

6) 62.5%

7) 3

8) 3

9) 2

10) False, True, False

Cumulative Frequency

What Is Cumulative Frequency?

Cumulative frequency is the mathematical way of describing a running total.

The cumulative frequency would add together all the values that are equal to or lower than the value in question. If, for example, you were calculating a cumulative frequency for the GCSE grades achieved by students, when you come to Grade C, you would also include the students who got a D, those who got an E and so on. You would actually be calculating the number of students who got a C or lower.

An example of cumulative frequencies is shown in this table:

Grade	Frequency	Cumulative Frequency
U	0	0
G	3	3
F	5	8
E	8	16
D	11	27
C	14	41
B	10	51
A	7	58
A*	2	60

Cumulative frequencies will often be shown on a graph for you to read off the values. Unlike most other graphs, cumulative frequency graphs will never decrease but each value will be the same as or more than the previous one.

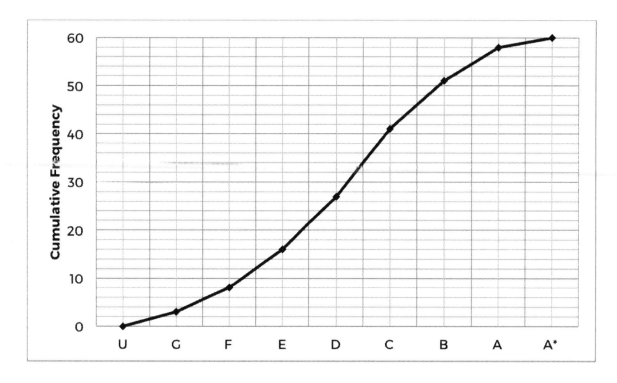

You can use this graph to work out how many students got a specific grade or below. For example, if you want to know how many got a grade D or below, you can follow the gridlines upwards from 'D' to the cumulative frequency line, and then follow the gridlines to the vertical axis to see what number of students it would correspond to. In this case, we can see that it is 27 (just as in the cumulative frequency table above).

Worked Example

A teacher produced a cumulative frequency graph (shown above) to show the GCSE grades achieved by 60 students. How many of those students got a grade B or lower?

Find grade B on the horizontal axis and look for the point on the line that is above this, then read off this value on the vertical axis.

This value is 51, meaning that there are 51 students that got grade B or lower.

Answer: 51

Top Tip

Questions on cumulative frequency sometimes contain inequality symbols. The larger end of the symbol always corresponds to the larger number (so x < 10 means that x is less than 10, and x > 10 means that x is greater than 10). When there is an additional line at the bottom of the symbol it means that the numbers could also be equal, so ≤ means 'less than or equal to' and ≥ means 'greater than or equal to'.

Using Cumulative Frequency

Although a cumulative frequency graph is designed to show you how many were equal to or less than a given value, you may be asked how many scored above a certain score. If, for example, you were asked how many scored above a grade B, you could work out how many got a B or below and then take this away from the total number, as all others must have got above a B.

You need to be careful whether the question is including the grade it mentions or not. Asking how many got a B or above is different to how many got above a B. If you are asked how many got a B or above you need to check how many got a C or below and take this from the total amount, as you want those who scored B to still be included in your answer.

Worked Example

A year 5 teacher produces a cumulative frequency graph to show the levels achieved by 30 students in English.

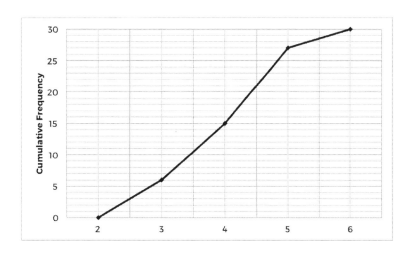

How many students achieved level 4 or above?

Look at how many didn't get 4 or above and take it away from the total of 30.

Since you are looking for those who scored below level 4, look up how many got 3 or below. Follow the gridline up from 3 and along to the vertical axis to see that this is 6 students.

Take this away from the total number to give 30 – 6 = 24 students as the final answer.

Answer: 24

Median and Quartiles From Cumulative Frequency Graphs

You could be asked to find the median or the quartiles from a cumulative frequency graph.

To find the median, work out half of the total number represented on the graph (the vertical axis), follow the gridlines along to your graph and then read off this value on the horizontal axis.

To work out the lower quartile, do the same with a quarter of the total number represented and for the upper quartile, use three quarters of the total number. If you are asked to find the interquartile range you need to subtract the lower quartile from the upper quartile.

Worked Example

A year 5 teacher produces a cumulative frequency graph to show the levels achieved by 30 students in English.

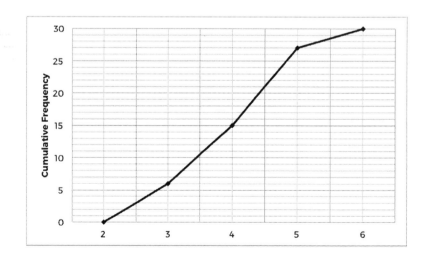

What is the median level?

To find the median, start by working out what is half of the total number of students. As the total is 30, this would be 15 students.

Find 15 on the vertical axis and follow the gridline along to the cumulative frequency graph. Then follow the gridline down from the point to the horizontal axis and read off the value of the median.

In this case, the median is level 4.

Answer: 4

Worked Example

A school produces a cumulative frequency graph showing the percentage scores of a group of students in an exam.

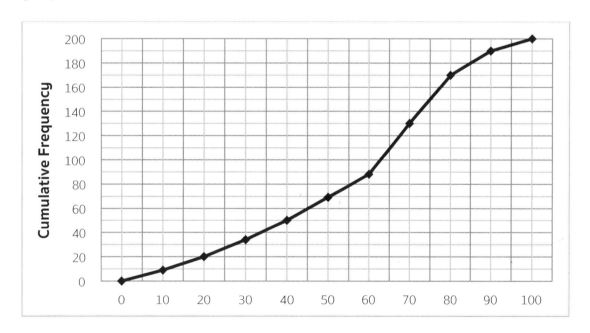

What is the interquartile range of the scores?

One quarter of 200 is 50, so to find the lower quartile look at the value of 50 on the vertical axis and read this off to find a value on the horizontal axis. This gives an answer of 40.

Three quarters of 200 is 150, so to find the upper quartile look at the value of 150 on the vertical axis and read this off to find a value on the horizontal axis. This gives an answer of 75.

The interquartile range is the difference between these two values.

75 – 40 = 35

Answer: 35

Practice Questions on Cumulative Frequency

Question 1

A sixth-form college produces a cumulative frequency graph to show the results of their students in A-Level History.

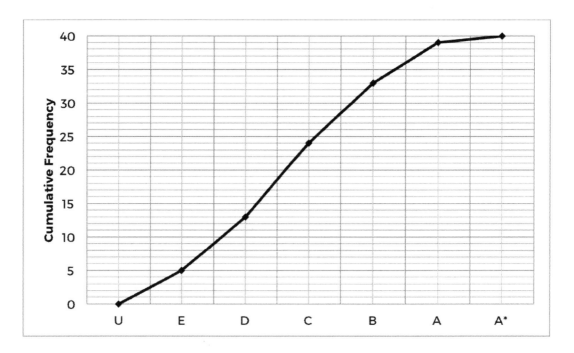

How many students achieved grade C or above?

Question 2

The following table shows the levels achieved by a group of year 9s in Spanish.

Level	2	3	4	5	6	7
Cumulative Frequency	1	2	10	24	29	31

What is the median level?

Question 3

The following table shows the levels achieved by a group of year 9s in Spanish.

Level	2	3	4	5	6	7
Cumulative Frequency	1	2	10	24	29	31

How many students scored between level 3 and level 5?

Question 4

A group of year 5s did a mental arithmetic test consisting of 10 questions. Their results were plotted as a cumulative frequency graph.

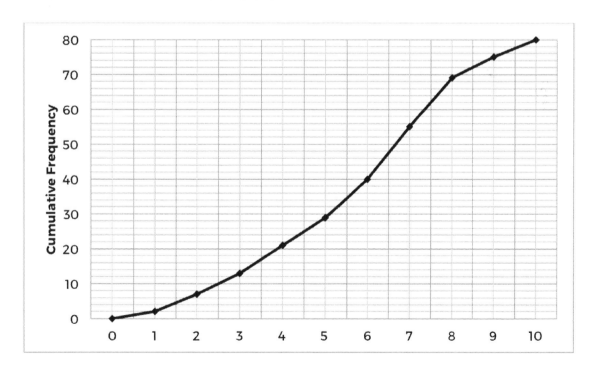

Indicate all true statements:

- Half of the students scored between 6 and 8.

- 5% of students scored full marks.

- The median score was 6.

Question 5

This graph shows the predicted science grades of a group of year 10 students.

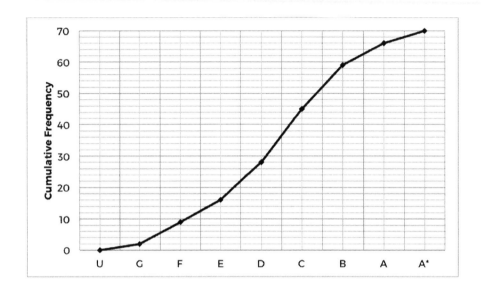

What percentage of students was predicted to get a grade C or above?

Question 6

This cumulative frequency graph compares the English levels of a group of students at the end of year 6 with the levels of the same group of students at the end of year 9.

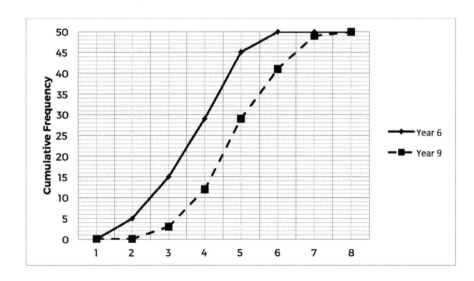

Indicate all true statements:

- There was a greater range of values in year 9 than in year 6.

- 10% of the year 6 students were level 6.

- There were as many year 9s that were level 5 as year 6s that were level 4.

Question 7

A school produces a cumulative frequency graph to show the number of A*-C grades achieved at GCSE by a group of students.

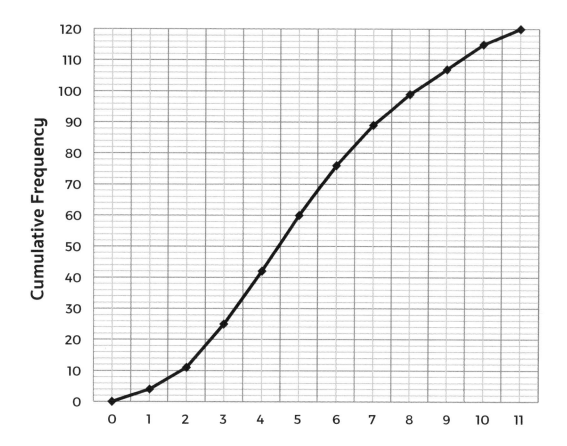

What percentage of students achieved 5 or more A*-C grades?

Question 8

A school recorded the levels that a group of students achieved at the end of Key Stage 2 in English.

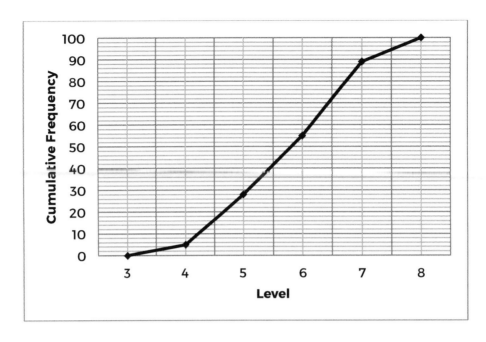

How many students achieved level 6 or above?

Question 9

Seventy students took a verbal reasoning test and their percentage scores were recorded in a cumulative frequency graph.

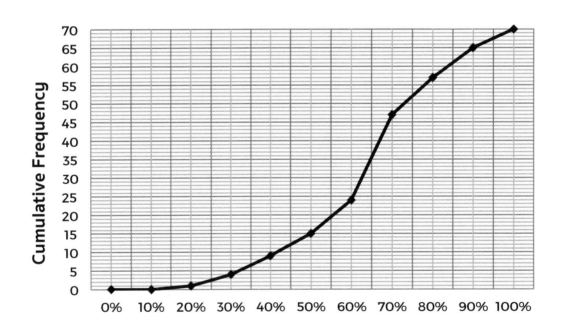

What was the median score?

Question 10

A sixth-form college records the grades achieved by students in an Psychology A-Level on a cumulative frequency graph.

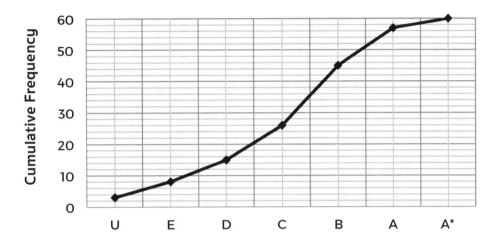

Indicate all true statements:

- Half of students got either a B or a C.

- The modal grade was C.

- Three students got A*

Solutions

Fully worked solutions to all of these questions can be accessed at www.qtsskillstests.com/cumulative

On-Screen Questions

1) 27

2) Level 5

3) 23

4) True, False, True

5) 60%

6) True, True, False

7) 65%

8) 72

9) 65%

10) True, False, True

Box & Whisker Plots

Using Box & Whisker Plots

In some questions you will be given information in a box and whisker plot (sometimes just called a 'box plot'). As its name suggests, this consists of a box with whiskers extending from each end.

The box and whisker plot contains 5 pieces of information:

- The minimum value

- The lower quartile

- The median

- The upper quartile

- The maximum value

Each of these is represented by a different part of the diagram.

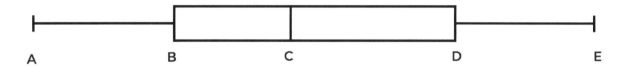

As you can see from the diagram, there are 5 distinct points marked A to E: the 2 ends of the whiskers, the 2 ends of the box, and the line in the centre of the box.

The diagram can be either horizontal or vertical, and will be lined up with an axis, such that a numerical value can be read for each of these points.

Each point corresponds to one of the 5 pieces of information listed above.

- Point A – The minimum value (the low end of the whisker).

- Point B – The lower quartile (the low end of the box)

- Point C – The median (the line inside the box)

- Point D – The upper quartile (the high end of the box)

- Point E – The maximum value (the high end of the whisker)

Remember that the median is the value that half of the students scored above and half of them scored below. The lower and upper quartiles are the values that one-quarter of students and three-quarters of students respectively scored below.

If you are asked to calculate the interquartile range, you can do so by subtracting the lower quartile from the upper quartile.

When you are given a box & whisker plot, it can be helpful to write out the 5 values the diagram shows, to use in any calculations you need to perform.

For example, consider the box and whisker diagram below.

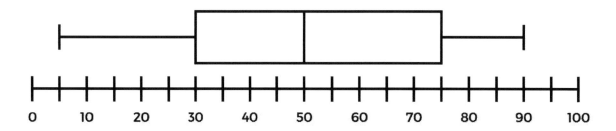

A great first step would be to read off each of the 5 values, which would then give you the data to work out whatever you are asked:

- The minimum value is 5

- The lower quartile is 30

- The median is 50

- The upper quartile is 75

- The highest value is 90

Worked Example

The percentage results of a group of students in a French test are shown in a box and whisker plot.

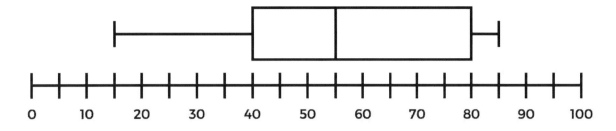

What is the interquartile range of the scores?

Start by reading off the data from the box and whisker plot.

The minimum value is 15%, the lower quartile is 40%, the median is 55%, the upper quartile is 80%, and the maximum value is 85%.

To work out the interquartile range, subtract the lower quartile from the upper quartile.

80% – 40% = 40%.

Answer: 40%

Top Tip

An easy mistake to make is to think that the median needs to be halfway between the quartiles, or halfway between the minimum and maximum values. This is not the case. In the worked example above, the difference between the lower quartile and the median is 15%, and the difference between the median and upper quartile is 25%. Though both sections represent the same number of students, this does not necessarily correspond to the same number of marks.

You may be asked a question about the percentage (or number) of students who scored between certain scores. It is important to remember that exactly 25% of students scored between the minimum and the lower quartile, another 25% between the lower quartile and the median, a further 25% between the median and the upper quartile, and the final 25% scored between the upper quartile and the maximum score.

Sometimes you will be asked to compare 2 or more box and whisker plots, or compare data from a box and whisker plot with data from another graph or chart (e.g. a cumulative frequency graph). In this case, if you read off and record the relevant values, the comparison can be made in a straightforward way.

Once you get used to box and whisker diagrams, you may be able to compare them by eye. For instance, you could notice which has the median in a higher location, or look to see which box is longest to compare interquartile range (or which plot is longest overall to compare range).

Practice Questions on Box & Whisker Plots

Question 1

Box and whisker plots are constructed to show the percentage attendance of students at each of 2 local primary schools.

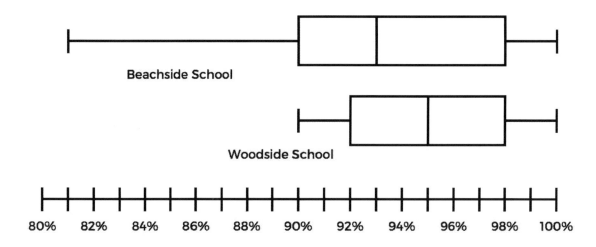

Given that 120 pupils attend each school, how many students altogether had an attendance of less than 90%?

Question 2

The Maths department of a school produced a series of box and whisker diagrams to show the performance of different Y9 sets in an end of year test.

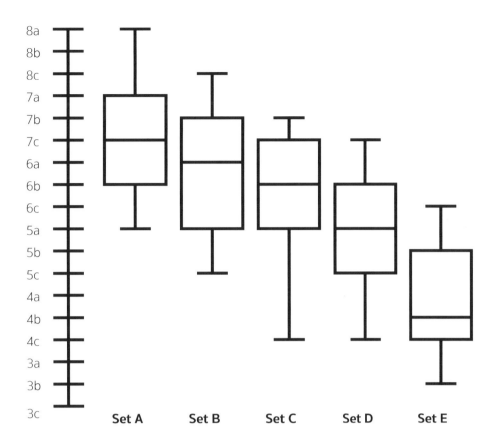

Indicate all true statements:

* The best achieving student in set E did better than the worst achieving student in set A.

* Set B had the greatest interquartile range.

* A quarter of students in set C got level 4C or lower.

Question 3

The percentage scores of a group of students in a Geography test are shown on the box and whisker plot below.

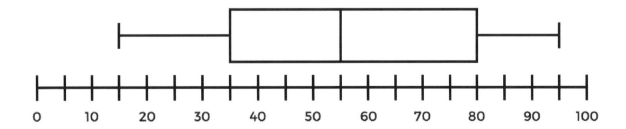

Three students took the test late and have not yet been added to the diagram.

Their scores were 12%, 38% and 53%.

What will be the range when these new results are included?

Question 4

The scores achieved by a group of 240 year 7s in their end-of-year tests in Maths, English and Science are shown on the box and whisker plot below.

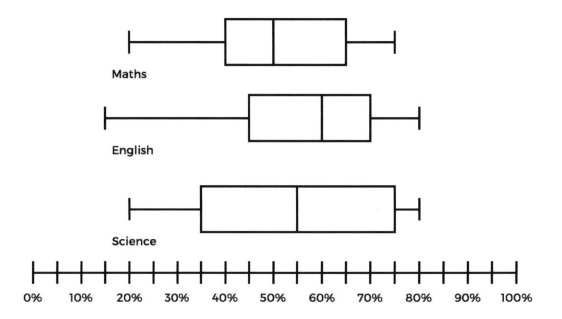

Indicate all true statements:

* The range in Science was higher than in any other subject.
* The interquartile range was the same in Maths as in English.
* 60 students scored between 40% and 50% in Maths.

Question 5

The scores of a group of A-Level students in an Economics exam are shown below:

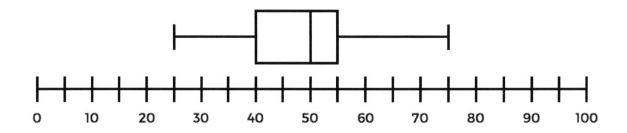

Indicate all true statements:

- 50% of the students scored between 25 and 50 marks.

- 50% of the students scored between 40 and 55 marks.

- 50% of the students scored between 55 and 75 marks.

Question 6

The percentage of year 6 students at different schools that achieved level 6 in English is plotted on a box and whisker plot.

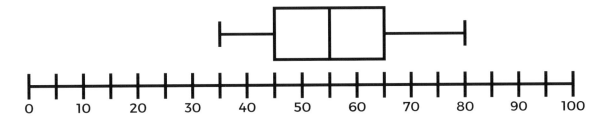

Altogether, there were 180 schools included in the data.

How many of the schools were within 25 percentage points of the best achieving school?

Question 7

In a secondary school, the English department plotted percentage scores in a test using a box and whisker plot.

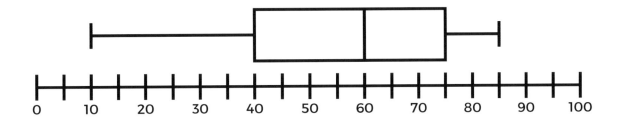

The Maths department at the same school plotted percentage scores of the same students using a cumulative Frequency diagram.

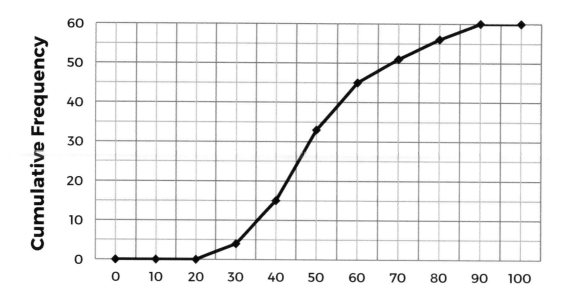

By how many percentage points was the interquartile range higher in English than in Maths?

Question 8

The percentage attendance of students in a school is monitored over two terms and displayed in a box and whisker plot.

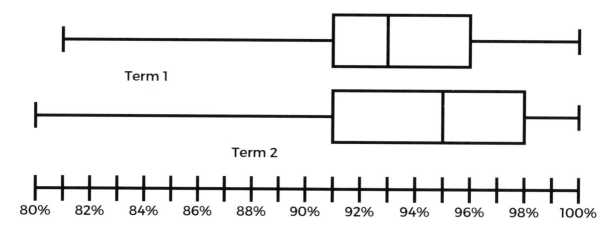

The school sets a target of maintaining the same rate of improvement in median attendance for Term 3.

In order to meet the target, what will the median attendance need to be in term 3?

Question 9

The results of a group of 220 year 11 students in a French test are shown on a box and whisker plot.

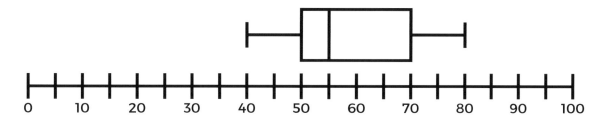

The grade boundaries are shown on the table below.

A*	A	B	C	D	E	F	G
89%	78%	64%	55%	47%	41%	32%	20%

How many students achieved grade C or above?

Question 10

This box and whisker plot shows the percentage scores of a group of 28 students on a verbal reasoning test.

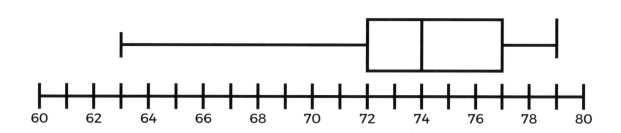

Indicate all true statements:

- 40% of students scored 70 marks or fewer.
- The highest score was 77.
- At least 10 students scored 74 or more marks.

Solutions

Fully worked solutions to all of these questions can be accessed at www.qtsskillstests.com/boxplots

On-Screen Questions

1) 30

2) True, True, False

3) 83%

4) False, True, True

5) True, True, False

6) 90

7) 15

8) 97%

9) 110

10) False, False, True

Practice Test 1

Mental Arithmetic Section

This section of the test is made up of twelve mental arithmetic questions to be answered under timed conditions. You must answer without using a calculator, though you are allowed to use a whiteboard for your workings.

For the best effect, ask somebody to read the questions aloud for you. Read each question twice, and then allow eighteen seconds to work out your answer.

Question 1

A child scored thirteen out of twenty on a spelling test. What percentage was this?

Question 2

In a class of twenty-seven children, each child raises twenty-five pence for charity. If the class are hoping to raise twenty pounds altogether, how much money do they still need to raise?

Question 3

What is three hundred and twenty five divided by zero point five?

Question 4

Out of a class of twenty-eight children, four of them were absent one day. What fraction of the class was present? Give your answer in its lowest terms.

Question 5

The area of a triangle is found by multiplying the base by the height and then dividing the answer by two. What is the area of a triangle with base seventeen centimetres and height fifteen centimetres?

Question 6

A school day starts at oh-eight forty-five. The morning session is made up of three lessons, each lasting fifty-five minutes, plus a twenty minute break. What time will the lunch break be?

Question 7

A teacher drives fourteen miles each way to a conference. If he is entitled to claim forty-five pence for each mile, how much can he claim altogether?

Question 8

On a piece of coursework, a student scored seventy-seven marks out of a possible one hundred and forty. What percentage is this?

Question 9

A teacher has six packs of eighteen pencils, and an additional five loose pencils. How many pencils does she have altogether?

Question 10

A student who receives additional numeracy support is given a forty minute intervention every day for a six week half term. How many hours of support is this?

Question 11

If a car is travelling at a speed of fifty-two miles per hour, how many miles would it travel in fifteen minutes?

Question 12

A student scored sixteen marks out of forty on an exam. They were allowed to re-sit the exam and improved their score by seventy-five per cent. What was their score on the re-sit?

On-Screen Section

This section of the test is made up of sixteen on-screen questions for which you will be allowed the use of a calculator as well as your whiteboard. Seven of the questions focus on interpreting and using written data, whilst the other nine are about solving written arithmetic problems. There is no time limit for the individual questions, but the whole test (including the mental arithmetic section) has a limit of 48 minutes, leaving around 36 minutes for this section.

Question 1

The following bar chart shows the levels achieved in Maths, English and Science by a cohort of students.

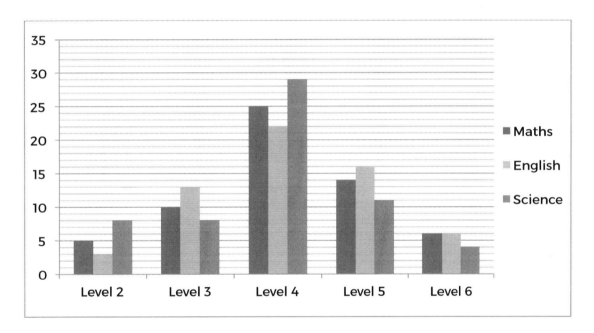

Indicate all true statements.

- Maths had a higher number of students achieving level 4 or above than any other subject.
- 25% of students achieved level 5 or above in Science.
- 10% of students achieved level 2 in Maths.

Question 2

The money raised by a school production is split between funding a school trip and a donation to charity in the ratio 3:4.

The money raised from various elements of the production is shown below.

	Money Raised
Ticket Sales	£238.50
Refreshment Sales	£51.75
Raffle	£82.00
Donations	£40.75

How much money was donated to charity?

Question 3

The money raised by a school production is split between funding a school trip and a donation to charity in the ratio 3:4.

The money raised from various elements of the production is shown below.

	Money Raised
Ticket Sales	£238.50
Refreshment Sales	£51.75
Raffle	£82.00
Donations	£40.75

Tickets cost £3 for adults and £1.50 for children.

27 children came to the production.

What was the total attendance?

Question 4

In London, the exchange rate between pounds and euros is £1 = €1.64, and in Paris the rate is €1 = 59p.

On a school trip, a group converts £275 into Euros in London. They then spend 70% of their money on the trip and convert the rest back into pounds in Paris.

To the nearest penny, how much money do they have left at the end of the trip?

Question 5

The scores achieved by 152 year 10s in their mock English Language and English Literature exams are shown in the box and whisker diagrams below.

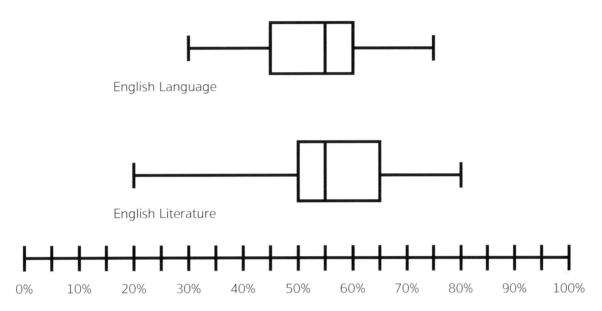

What is the interquartile range of the scores in English Language?

Question 6

The scores achieved by 152 year 10s in their mock English Language and English Literature exams are shown in the box and whisker diagrams below.

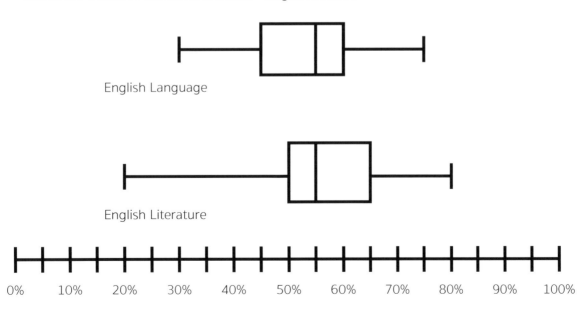

Students needed to achieve 65% or above to get a grade C.

How many students achieved grade C or above in English Literature?

Question 7

The percentage scores of 10 students in a spelling test are shown below.

Student	Score
Amy	52%
Blake	69%
Charlie	67%
Daniel	57%
Emma	75%
Frankie	65%
Georgina	45%
Harriet	65%
Iwan	47%
Josh	56%

What is the median score?

Question 8

A teacher has appointments booked to see parents during a progress day.

Each parent of a year 7 child is allotted a 15-minute slot with the teacher.

Parents of other children are allotted a 5-minute slot.

The progress day starts at 09:20 and the teacher needs to see 13 parents of year 7 children and take a 30-minute lunch break.

If the day finishes at 15:25, how many other parents can the teacher see?

Question 9

A Maths department plotted the end of KS3 levels of 150 students on a cumulative frequency diagram.

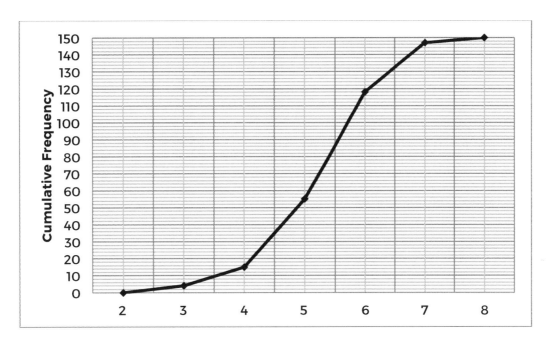

The department invited all students who were level 5 or 6 to a summer school.

How many students were invited?

Question 10

An English course requires students to submit 5 pieces of coursework.

The piece with the lowest percentage score is disregarded and the mean percentage score of the other 4 pieces is calculated as the overall score for the course.

The scores a student achieved on each of the pieces of coursework is shown below.

	A	B	C	D	E
Marks Scored	34	29	41	23	30
Total Marks Available	50	50	50	50	50

What was the overall score of this student?

Question 11

A Maths department produced a scatter graph to compare the performance of a group of students in a calculator exam and in a non-calculator exam.

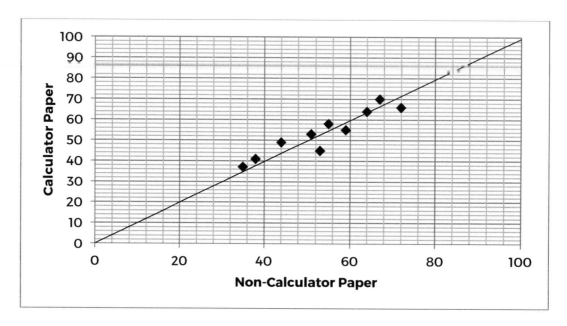

Indicate all true statements:

- The majority of students did better on the calculator paper than the non-calculator paper.
- There was a greater range of scores on the non-calculator paper than on the calculator paper.
- One student achieved identical scores on both papers.

Question 12

A sixth form tutor is arranging a Christmas celebration for students.

The total cost is calculated using the following formula.

Cost = £270 + (number of students × £12)

If the sixth form sell tickets to students for £15, how many students will need to attend in order for the event to break even?

Question 13

A school produced pie charts to show the percentages of students in years 10 & 11 studying different humanities subjects.

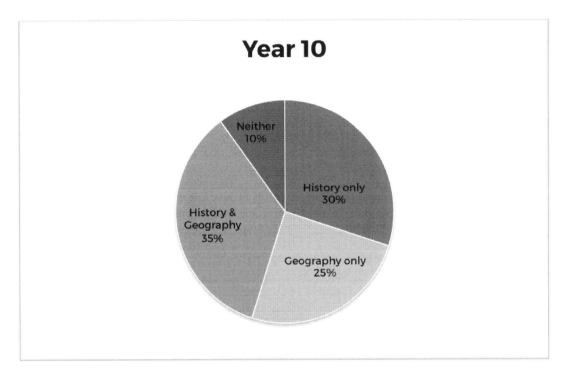

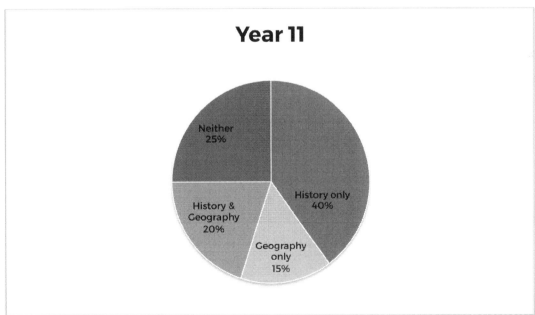

What is the percentage point decrease in the number of students studying history from year 10 to year 11?

Question 14

A school trip to France is planned for 13 students and 3 members of staff in a school minibus.

The trip involves driving 90 miles in the UK and 200 kilometres in France.

5 miles = 8 kilometres.

The fuel consumption of the minibus is 7 miles to the litre, and each litre of petrol costs £1.23.

If the total cost of the trip is the cost of fuel plus £45 per person for the ferry crossing, what will the overall cost be (to the nearest penny)?

Question 15

A P.E. department tracked the average score of a class on a bleep test over 5 P.E. lessons, and also plotted the scores of one student on that graph with black dots.

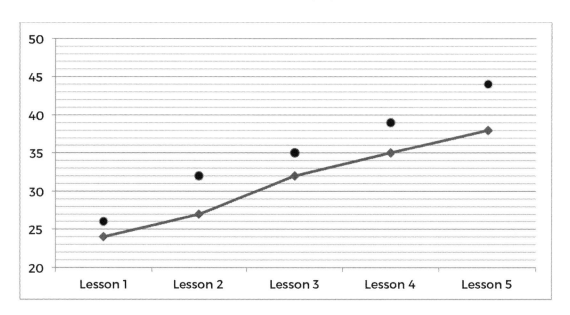

On average, how much was the student above the class average?

Question 16

In a science exam, the Physics and Biology sections are each weighted at 30% and the Chemistry section is weighted at 40%.

The scores a student achieved in each of the sections is shown below.

	Physics	**Biology**	**Chemistry**
Marks Achieved	19	27	36
Total Marks Available	50	50	50

What was their overall percentage score for the exam?

Give your answer to one decimal place.

Solutions

Fully worked solutions to all of these questions can be accessed at www.qtsskillstests.com/practice-tests

Mental Arithmetic Questions

1) 65%

2) £13.25

3) 650

4) $^6/_7$

5) 127.5cm^2

6) 11:50

7) £12.60

8) 55%

9) 113

10) 20 hours

11) 13 miles

12) 28

On-Screen Questions

1) True, True, False

2) £236

3) 93

4) £79.83

5) 15%

6) 38

7) 61%

8) 28

9) 103

10) 67%

11) True, True, True

12) 90

13) 5%

14) £757.76

15) 4

16) 56.4%

Practice Test 2

Mental Arithmetic Section

This section of the test is made up of twelve mental arithmetic questions to be answered under timed conditions. You must answer without using a calculator, though you are allowed to use a whiteboard for your workings.

For the best effect, ask somebody to read the questions aloud for you. Read each question twice, and then allow eighteen seconds to work out your answer.

Question 1

Out of a class of twenty-nine students, a teacher forms seven groups of three. How many students are left over?

Question 2

Sixty students in a school of two hundred and fifty participated in a school play. What percentage of the total number of students participated in the play?

Question 3

Using a conversion of one kilogram equals two point two pounds, convert twelve kilograms into pounds.

Question 4

A teacher attends three training days and is paid mileage for each. If the journey is eleven miles each way and the teacher can claim thirty-five pence per mile, how much can be claimed in total?

Question 5

What is forty-five per cent as a fraction in its lowest terms?

Question 6

What is ninety-four divided by twenty?

Question 7

How many five centimetre strips can be cut from a piece of card two point seven metres long?

Question 8

In a parents evening, a teacher needs to see each parent for five minutes and will take a ten minute break after seeing each ten parents. If there are twenty-six parents to see and the evening begins at fifteen thirty, what time will it finish?

Question 9

Two ninths of the children in a junior school are invited on a trip. If there are one hundred and twenty-six children in the school, how many children are invited?

Question 10

If a teacher has ninety Euros and converts it back into pounds at a rate of sixty pence for every Euro, how much money will she end up with?

Question 11

A school trip arrives at a museum at eleven forty-five am. The children are given a tour that lasts thirty-five minutes; they spend twenty minutes looking at an exhibit and have lunch for fifty minutes. The rest of the time they are free to look around the museum. If they set off back to school at three pm, how long did they have to look around?

Question 12

A piece of computer equipment is advertised as costing four hundred and fifty pounds plus fifteen per cent tax. How much will it cost in total?

On-Screen Section

This section of the test is made up of sixteen on-screen questions and you will be allowed the use of a calculator as well as your whiteboard. Seven of the questions focus on interpreting and using written data, whilst the other nine are about solving written arithmetic problems. There is no time limit for the individual questions, but the whole test (including the mental arithmetic section) has a limit of 48 minutes, leaving around 36 minutes for this section.

Question 1

The 168 students in year 8 were split between food technology and resistant materials in the ratio 5:3.

How many students studied resistant materials?

Question 2

A Psychology department made a pie chart to show the results of 40 students in an A-Level exam.

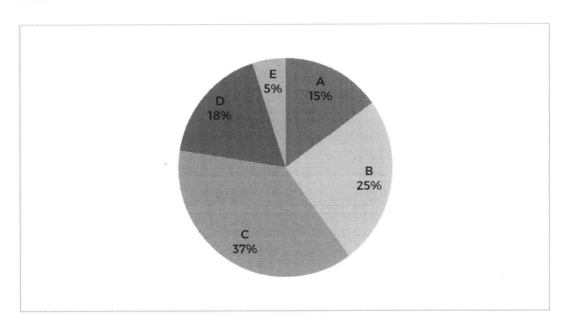

How many students got a B or above?

Question 3

This table shows the languages that year 9 students at two schools chose to study.

School	French	German	Spanish
Beachside School	22	18	15
Hillside School		17	22

The proportion of students that studied French was the same at both schools.

How many students studied French at Hillside School?

Question 4

A cumulative frequency graph is produced to track how many GCSEs with grades A*-C students at a school achieved.

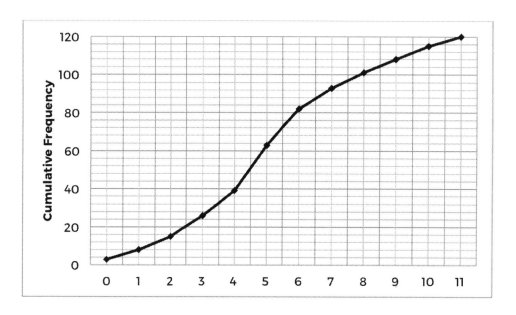

How many students achieved 5 or more A*-C grades?

Question 5

The overall score for an English course is found from the coursework score (C) and the exam score (E), weighted according to the following formula.

Total Score = [3C + E] ÷ 4

What was the overall score of a student who scored 71 on their coursework and 59 on the exam?

Question 6

In a primary school charity fundraiser, the amount raised by each class is shown below along with the number of students in the class.

Class	Number of Students	Amount Raised
Reception	24	£18.24
Year 1	28	£25.57
Year 2	27	£27.95
Year 3	29	£33.66
Year 4	31	£46.12
Year 5	28	£43.80
Year 6	27	£50.06

To the nearest penny, what is the mean amount of money raised by each student in the school?

Question 7

The chart below shows the percentage of students in three different year groups that chose to participate in football, hockey and netball in sporting inter-form activities.

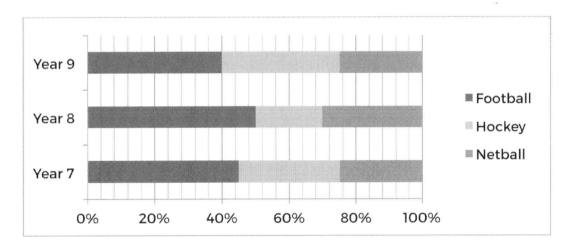

There were 180 students in each year group.

How many students in total participated in the hockey?

Question 8

In a school sports day, a student runs 800m in 120 seconds. What is this speed in miles per hour?

Question 9

The level achieved in English at the end of Key Stage 3 by a cohort of students is shown in the table below.

Level	3	4	5	6	7	8
Number of Students	4	15	33	49	28	6

What is the mean level? Give your answer to 2 decimal places.

Question 10

The level achieved in English at the end of Key Stage 3 by a cohort of students is shown in the table below.

Level	3	4	5	6	7	8
Number of Students	4	15	33	49	28	6

What is the median level?

Question 11

A school tracked the membership of 2 extra-curricular activities over a 5-year period on a line graph.

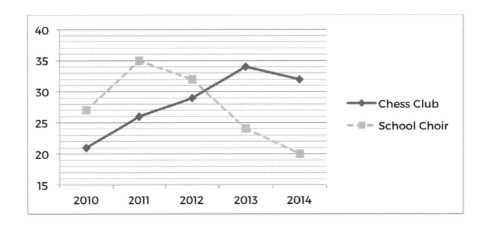

Indicate all true statements:

- The chess club grew each year.
- The mean membership of the choir was higher than the mean membership of the chess club.
- The range of the number of students signed up for the two activities was the same.

Question 12

This table shows the reading ages in years and months (where 8-9 means 8 years, 9 months) of 12 students measured each month through a school year.

Student	Sept	Oct	Nov	Dec	Jan	Feb	Mar	Apr	May	Jun	Jul
A	8-9	8-10	8-10	8-11	9-0	9-1	9-2	9-3	9-4	9-5	9-6
B	8-2	8-3	8-4	8-5	8-6	8-7	8-8	8-9	8-10	8-11	9-1
C	8-6	8-5	8-6	8-6	8-7	8-8	8-8	8-9	8-10	9-0	9-1
D	9-1	9-3	9-5	9-7	9-9	9-11	10-1	10-3	10-5	10-7	10-9
E	7-5	7-7	7-8	7-9	7-9	7-10	7-11	8-0	8-2	8-3	8-4
F	8-0	8-1	8-2	8-3	8-4	8-5	8-6	8-6	8-8	8-9	8-10
G	8-8	8-9	8-10	9-0	9-2	9-3	9-5	9-6	9-7	9-8	9-10
H	8-6	8-7	8-8	8-9	8-11	9-0	9-1	9-2	9-4	9-5	9-7
I	8-3	8-4	8-5	8-6	8-7	8-8	8-9	8-10	8-11	9-0	9-1
J	8-11	9-0	9-0	9-1	9-2	9-3	9-5	9-6	9-7	9-9	9-10
K	7-10	7-11	8-0	8-1	8-1	8-2	8-3	8-3	8-4	8-5	8-6
L	9-0	9-1	9-2	9-4	9-5	9-6	9-8	9-9	9-10	9-11	10-0

Which student(s) showed a trend of consistent improvement?

Question 13

The percentage scores of 92 students in a Physics test are shown on the box plot below.

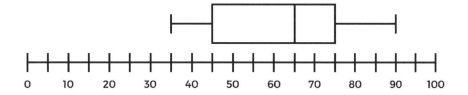

How many students scored between 25% and 45% on the test?

Question 14

A school produces a cumulative frequency graph to show the end of KS2 results of a group of students in English and Maths.

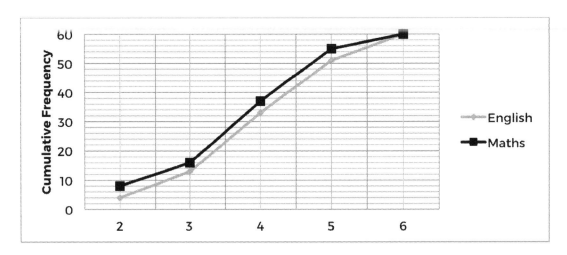

Indicate all true statements.

- The same number of students achieved level 5 in both subjects.
- There was a greater range of scores in English than in Maths.
- 15% of students got level 6 in Maths.

Question 15

A teacher works out how long they can spend with each parent at a parents evening by dividing 180 by the number of parents they need to see and rounding the answer up to the nearest minute.

If the teacher needs to see 24 parents and they start the parents evening at 16:00, what time will they finish?

Question 16

As part of an entrance exam, a school gave a group of children two tests, one in verbal reasoning and the other in non-verbal reasoning and plotted their results on a scatter diagram.

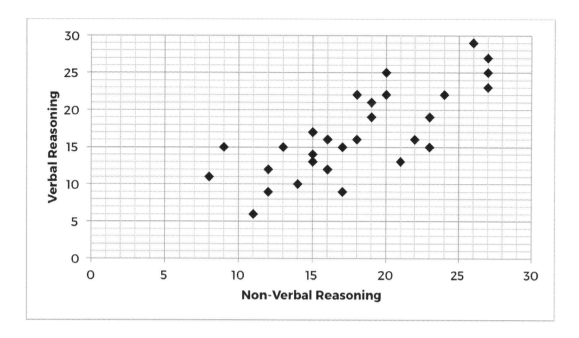

What proportion of children scored higher on the non-verbal reasoning test?

Give your answer as a decimal to two decimal places.

Solutions

Fully worked solutions to all of these questions can be accessed at www.qtsskillstests.com/practice-tests

Mental Arithmetic Questions

1) 8

2) 24%

3) 26.4lbs

4) £23.10

5) $^9/_{20}$

6) 4.7

7) 54

8) 18:00

9) 28

10) £54

11) 1 hour, 30 minutes

12) £517.50

On-Screen Questions

1) 63

2) 16

3) 26

4) 81

5) 68

6) £1.26

7) 153

8) 15 miles per hour

9) 5.74

10) 6

11) False, False, False

12) Students D & I

13) 23

14) True, False, False

15) 19:12

16) 0.55

Practice Test 3

Mental Arithmetic Section

This section of the test is made up of twelve mental arithmetic questions to be answered under timed conditions. You must answer without using a calculator, though you are allowed to use a whiteboard for your workings.

For the best effect, ask somebody to read the questions aloud for you. Read each question twice, and then allow eighteen seconds to work out your answer.

Question 1

A teacher completes a twenty-eight mile journey and is able to claim expenses of forty pence per mile. How much can she claim in total?

Question 2

How many twelve minute individual performances could a teacher fit into a lesson lasting an hour and three quarters?

Question 3

Out of twenty-seven students in a class, twenty-one had brought a packed lunch and the rest stayed for a school dinner. What fraction of the class stayed for school dinner? Give your answer in its lowest terms.

Question 4

In each eight kilometres there are five miles. How many miles are in ninety-six kilometres?

Question 5

If each child uses three exercise books in a year, how many books will be needed for three classes with twenty-five children in each?

Question 6

A teacher needs to convert sixty pounds into Euros at an exchange rate of one point six Euros for every one pound. How many Euros will he receive?

Question 7

A student scored forty-two marks out of sixty on a French test. What percentage is this?

Question 8

There are one hundred and fifty three children in year seven and one hundred and sixty five children in year eight. How many groups of six children can be made from these year groups?

Question 9

A child took three mental arithmetic tests, each with a total of twenty marks available. If he scored eleven and thirteen on the first two tests, how many did he need to score on the third test to achieve an overall percentage of fifty per cent?

Question 10

A school trip is due back at school for fifteen thirty and set off at fourteen hundred. The total distance for the journey is sixty miles. What speed (in miles per hour) will the coach need to travel to get back to school on time?

Question 11

One child has a reading age of eight years and six months whilst another child has a reading age of five years and nine months. What is the difference in months between the reading ages of these two children?

Question 12

In a school of three hundred and seventy-five students, it is decided that the top twenty per cent will be given a gold award. How many students are given a gold award?

On-Screen Section

This section of the test is made up of sixteen on-screen questions and you will be allowed the use of a calculator as well as your whiteboard. Seven of the questions focus on interpreting and using written data, whilst the other nine are about solving written arithmetic problems. There is no time limit for the individual questions, but the whole test (including the mental arithmetic section) has a limit of 48 minutes, leaving around 36 minutes for this section.

Question 1

A school tracked the percentage of students that left with 5 or more A*-C GCSE grades including English and Maths over a 6 year period.

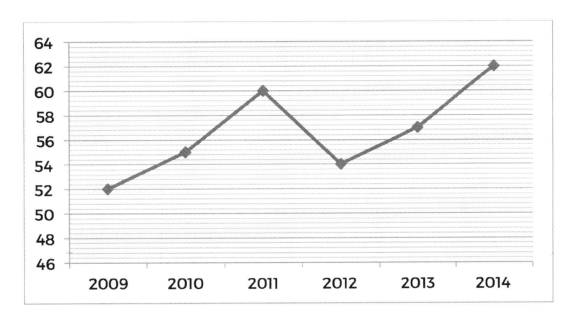

What was the mean percentage of students that achieved this?

Give your answer to 1 decimal place.

Question 2

A school has staggered the lunch break of children with an early lunch and a late lunch in a ratio 2:5.

There are 84 children who have an early lunch.

How many children are in the school altogether?

Question 3

A box and whisker plot is produced to show the end of KS2 levels achieved by 80 students in Maths, English and Science

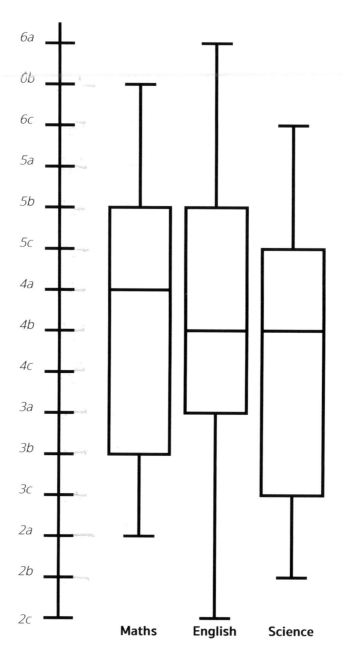

Indicate all true statements:

- The interquartile range was the same for English and Science.
- The range of scores was the same for Maths and Science.
- 40 students achieved level 4a or above in Maths.

Question 4

A school day begins at 08:50 and finishes at 14:45.

The day is made up of 5 lessons, a 50-minute lunch break, a 15-minute morning break and a 15-minute tutor time.

If a year 8 class spend 12% of their lesson time in English, how many hours and minutes do they spend in English over a 12 week term?

Question 5

A scatter diagram is produced to compare the scores children achieved in a French speaking test and a Science practical.

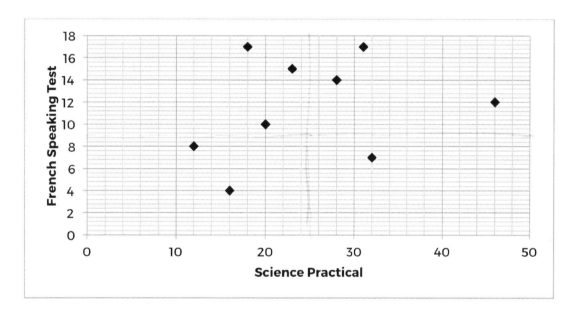

How many students scored above the median in both the French speaking test and the Science practical?

Question 6

A teacher is ordering new displays for his classroom.

The cost is calculated using the following formula, where C is the cost in pounds, L is the number of large display boards in the classroom, M is the number of medium display boards and S is the number of small display boards.

$$C = 29 + 12.5L + 8.5M + 6S$$

How much would it cost him if his classroom has 2 large display boards, 3 medium display boards and 5 small display boards?

Question 7

The table below shows the number of students achieving each grade in GCSE Maths at 3 different schools.

School	A*	A	B	C	D	E	F	G
Woodside School	8	12	19	22	21	16	9	3
Hillside School	6	14	18	25	32	20	15	6
Beachside School	7	9	26	24	15	11	5	1

Across all 3 schools, what percentage of students achieved a grade C or above?

Give your answer to the nearest whole number.

Question 8

The table below shows the number of students achieving each grade in GCSE Maths at 3 different schools.

School	A*	A	B	C	D	E	F	G
Woodside School	8	12	19	22	21	16	9	3
Hillside School	6	14	18	25	32	20	15	6
Beachside School	7	9	26	24	15	11	5	1

Which school had the highest percentage of students achieve a grade A* or A?

Question 9

A school produced pie charts to track the languages studied by their year 9 cohorts of 50 boys and 70 girls.

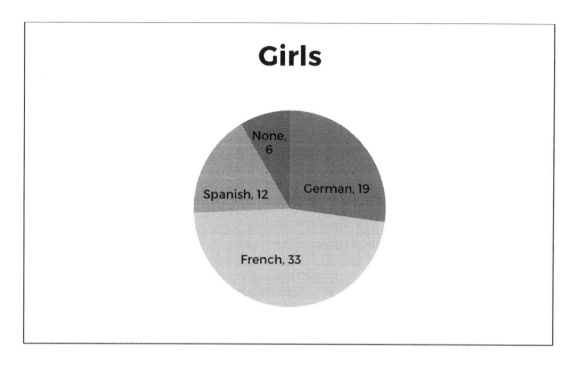

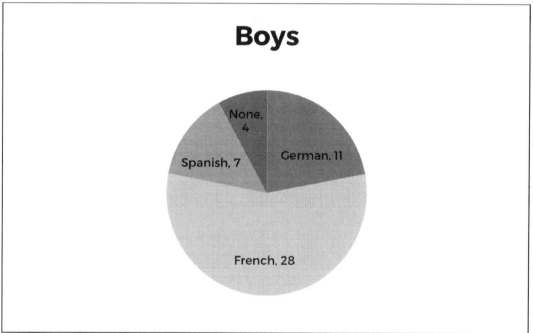

Indicate all true statements.

- A higher percentage of boys than girls study French.
- Exactly 5% of students don't study a language.
- A quarter of the students study German.

Question 10

An art teacher needs to order new supplies of coloured paper for her classroom.

There are three different suppliers that she could use.

Supplier	Price	Discount	Postage	Credit Card Charge
Classroom Supplies	8p per sheet	No Discount	£9.95	1.5%
The Art Store	9p per sheet	15% off orders above £200	£4.95	No Charge
Paper Inc.	10p per sheet	Every 5th sheet free	Free	1%

She wants to order 3000 sheets of paper. Which supplier should she use?

Question 11

A cumulative frequency graph is produced to track the percentage scores of 200 students on a mock exam.

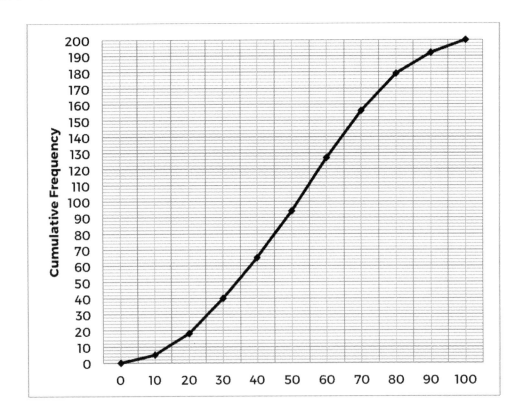

What is the interquartile range of the scores?

Question 12

The two papers on a History exam are weighted in the ratio 2:3.

What was the overall percentage score of a student who scored 53% on paper 1 and 63% on paper 2?

Question 13

The scale on a map says that 1cm represents 15 miles.

On that map, two towns are 7.5cm apart.

On a journey between those towns, a signpost says that the destination is 48 kilometres away.

Given that 5 miles = 8 kilometres, how far (in km) has already been travelled?

Question 14

This graph shows the number of students achieving each level in English at the end of Key Stage 3 in two different years.

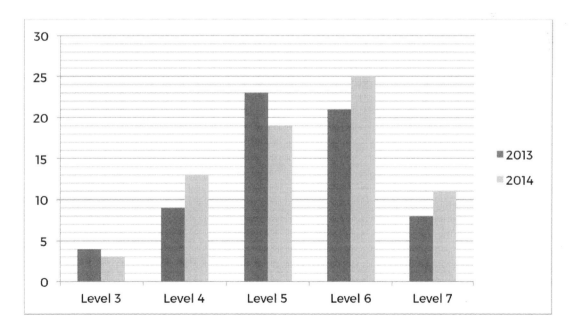

What was the modal level in 2014?

Question 15

This graph shows the levels achieved in English at the end of Key Stage 3 by 65 students in 2013 and 71 students in 2014.

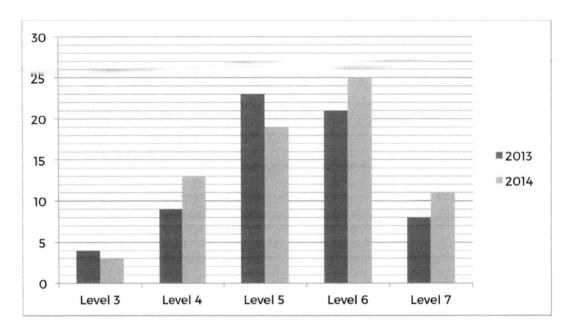

What was the difference in the percentage of students achieving level 6 or above in 2014 compared to 2013?

Give your answer to 1 decimal place.

Question 16

Four pupils took a mental arithmetic test.

The mean score was 11, the range was 3 and the mode was 10.

What were the four scores?

Solutions

Fully worked solutions to all of these questions can be accessed at www.qtsskillstests.com/practice-tests

Mental Arithmetic Questions

1) £11.20

2) 8

3) $^2/_9$

4) 60 miles

5) 225

6) €96

7) 70%

8) 53

9) 6

10) 40 miles per hour

11) 33 months

12) 75

On-Screen Questions

1) 56.7%

2) 294

3) False, True, True

4) 33

5) 2

6) £109.50

7) 55%

8) Woodside School

9) True, False, True

10) The Art Store

11) 34

12) 59%

13) 132km

14) Level 6

15) 6.1%

16) 10, 10, 11, 13

37351019R00145

Printed in Great Britain
by Amazon